EXPLORING THE HUMAN BODY

Reproduction and Growth

Michaela Miller

FRANKLIN WATTS
LONDON • SYDNEY

First published in 2005 by
Franklin Watts
96 Leonard Street
London EC2A 4XD

Franklin Watts Australia
Level 17/207 Kent Street
Sydney NSW 2000

Produced by Arcturus Publishing Ltd,
26/27 Bickels Yard, 151–153 Bermondsey Street, London SE1 3HA

© 2005 Arcturus Publishing

Series concept: Alex Woolf
Editor: Alex Woolf
Designer: Peta Morey
Artwork: Michael Courtney
Picture researcher: Glass Onion Pictures
Consultant: Dr Kristina Routh

Picture Credits
Corbis: 29 (Gideon Mendel).
La Leche League International: 20 (Suba Tidball).
Science Photo Library: 5 (Lea Paterson), 7 (BSIP, Laurent), 11 (Dr Yorgos Nikas),
13 (Ian Boddy), 15 (Dr G. Moscoso), 17 (Deep Light Productions), 18 (Ruth
Jenkinson/MIDIRS), 21 (Ian Hooton), 23 (BSIP, Laurent), 25 (Damien Lovegrove),
26 (Tek Image), 27 (BSIP, Laurent), 28 (Eye of Science).
Topfoto: 24 (John Powell).

Every attempt has been made to clear copyright. Should there be any
inadvertent omission, please apply to the publisher for rectification.

A CIP catalogue record for this book is available from the British Library

ISBN 0 7496 5962 9

Printed in Singapore

Contents

Creating Life

If living things stopped reproducing – creating new life – the world would become an empty place. All types of life, including plants, animals and bacteria, would soon die out.

Different creatures reproduce in different ways. The smallest creatures, like amoebae, simply split in half to create more amoebae. This way of reproducing is called asexual reproduction. Other living things need two sexes – a male and a female – to join together, before new life can be created. This is called sexual reproduction.

This diagram shows asexual reproduction. An amoeba – a single-celled creature – simply splits in two when it reaches a certain size.

Hatching or Birth?

Just as different creatures have different ways of reproducing, their babies have different ways of entering the world as well. Female mammals, such as humans, grow their babies inside their bodies until the babies are ready to be born. Most other animals, like birds, fish, amphibians, reptiles and insects, lay eggs. Their young stay in the eggs until they are ready to hatch.

Human Reproduction

Human reproduction, or sex, often seems more complicated than reproduction for the rest of the animal kingdom. This is because humans are highly complex and social creatures, and the way they go about reproducing usually involves strong feelings and emotions. Love, attraction, care and respect are just some of the positive feelings that can be associated with human reproduction.

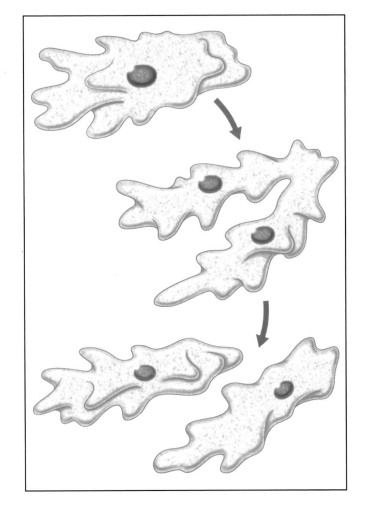

Human babies are produced through sexual reproduction.

As young people grow up and enter puberty – the stage when their bodies start to become more adult – they usually find themselves thinking more about sex and asking questions about it. This is all perfectly normal – if they did not have these feelings or curiosity, the human race would soon cease to exist.

However, like many other things, reproduction can have a negative side too. If people don't look after their bodies they can become ill and pass on diseases through having sex. If babies are born to parents who do not want them or cannot look after them properly, the babies will suffer and may even die. Also, if someone has sex before they are ready, they can suffer and feel bad too.

Case notes

How long does it take to reproduce?

The length of time it takes to reproduce depends on the type of animal. Human babies usually take around forty weeks to grow inside their mothers before they are ready to be born. An elephant pregnancy can last two years. Bird eggs can take anywhere between two and eleven weeks to hatch depending on the type of bird. Eggs from small birds take less time to hatch than eggs from a large bird like an albatross.

The Female Reproductive System

To reproduce, both females and males have reproductive organs. A woman's reproductive organs are tucked inside her body. They are connected to an opening between her legs called the vagina, or birth canal. The vagina is between two other openings: the anus, from which solid waste (faeces) leaves the body, and the urethra, which lets the liquid waste (urine) out.

The female reproductive organs also include two ovaries, two fallopian tubes and a uterus – also known as a womb. Each of these parts is needed to create life.

Ovaries are two rounded organs, about three centimetres long, that store hundreds of thousands of tiny eggs. These eggs are the female sex cells. Each egg – called an ovum – is about as big as a pencil dot. Although a girl's ovaries store hundreds of thousands of eggs, only about four hundred will be released during her lifetime.

This diagram shows how the female reproductive system is situated within the body.

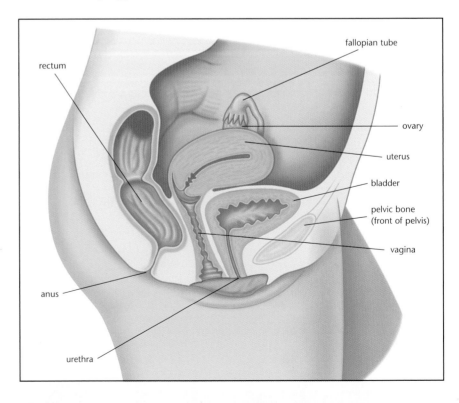

The Egg's Journey

Before a baby can start to form, an ovum must travel along a fallopian tube and successfully join with a male sex cell called a sperm. This joining is known as fertilization.

Eggs only start being released when the female reproductive organs are mature enough. This happens when a girl reaches puberty – usually in her early teens – when chemicals in her blood, known as hormones, tell the ovaries to release one egg. After that, an egg will be released each month, usually from alternate ovaries.

Before the egg is released, the uterus gets ready for the possible arrival of a fertilized egg by making a soft lining that is rich in blood vessels. If the egg is not fertilized, the lining is not needed. It breaks down, with the egg, into a few tablespoons of blood and leaves the body through the vagina.

Sometimes menstruation causes pain. Exercise, heat and pain-killing medicine can help, but anyone worried about period pain should see their doctor.

This bleeding happens about every 28 days and is called menstruation, or a period. During periods, girls and women usually use sanitary towels or tampons to stop the blood getting on their underwear. Most women stop menstruating when they reach about fifty, and they are no longer fertile. This is called the menopause.

Case notes

When do periods start?

Most girls start menstruating between the ages of eleven and thirteen, but some may start their periods as early as nine or as late as fifteen. This is all quite normal. Periods last from about three to eight days and usually happen every month, but they can happen more or less often than that.

The Male Reproductive System

The male reproductive organs – the penis and the testes (or testicles) – are outside a man's body and hang between his legs. The two testes are held and protected by a bag of skin called the scrotum.

Each testicle produces sperm – the male sex cells – usually beginning when a boy is between ten and twelve years old. The scrotum's job is to keep the testes at the right temperature for sperm production. In the cold, the scrotum moves the testes close to the body to keep the sperm warm. In the heat it moves them further away from the body to keep the sperm cool.

Sperm are tiny cells visible only with a microscope. They have a tadpole shape, with a round head and long tail. Each sperm is about 0.05 millimetres long. The testes produce millions of sperm every day.

The Sperm's Journey

For reproduction to take place, sperm have to leave the body through the penis. To get there they first have to travel from the testes through a series of tubes. Each testicle

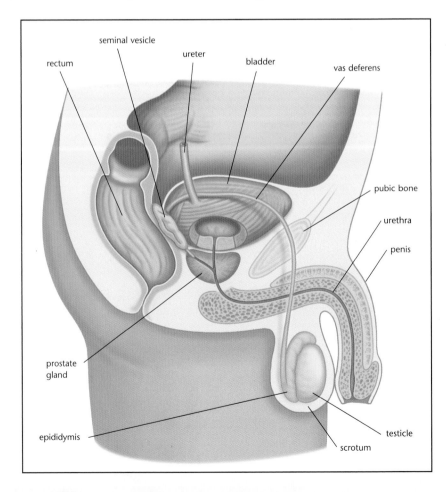

This diagram shows how the male reproductive system is situated within the body.

rectum

seminal vesicle

ureter

bladder

vas deferens

pubic bone

urethra

penis

prostate gland

epididymis

scrotum

testicle

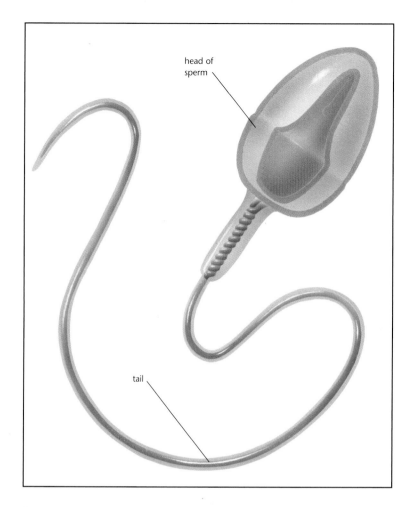

head of
sperm

tail

A highly magnified sperm. The head of
the sperm, which joins with the egg, is
moved along by the tail.

has its own set of tubes. The first set is called the
epididymis, which acts as a sperm storage area. The sperm
then travel through the next set of tubes, known as the vas
deferens. Here they start mixing with fluids produced by
the seminal vesicles and the prostate gland. This mixture of
fluid and sperm is called semen.

The semen travels up through a tube in the penis called
the urethra before emerging rapidly through an opening at
the tip of the penis. This is called ejaculation and usually
happens only when the penis is hard. This hardness is
known as an erection and it happens when men are
sexually excited.

The urethra also connects to the bladder where urine is
stored, but special muscles ensure that during an erection
and ejaculation, urine and semen do not come out of the
urethra at the same time.

Case notes

What is a wet dream?

Wet dreams are a common
sign that a boy has reached
puberty, and that his body is
now producing sperm. During
a wet dream a boy is normally
dreaming of something that
makes him sexually excited.
He then has an erection and
ejaculates semen which
makes his sheets or pyjamas
wet and sticky.

Creating a Baby

Before an egg can be fertilized and a baby created, a man's penis and a woman's vagina must join together. This joining is called sexual intercourse, sex or making love. Sexual intercourse usually happens privately when a man and woman feel very close and attracted to one another.

During sex, the man's penis becomes hard and erect and the woman's vagina becomes wet and slippery so that the penis can slide easily inside her. The man and woman then move together so that the penis slides in and out of the vagina.

This movement encourages the sperm and semen to start moving through the network of tubes in the man's scrotum and penis. Eventually the man's penis ejaculates and the sperm and semen enter the woman's vagina.

The Sperm Race

Each ejaculation contains between two and five million sperm. They all swim quickly, using their tadpole-like tails, to go up the vagina, into the uterus and towards the fallopian tubes. Each sperm races to join with the egg, or ovum. If they find the egg, the sperm surround it and try to burrow in to fertilize it. Only one sperm will be successful and join with the egg to start a new life.

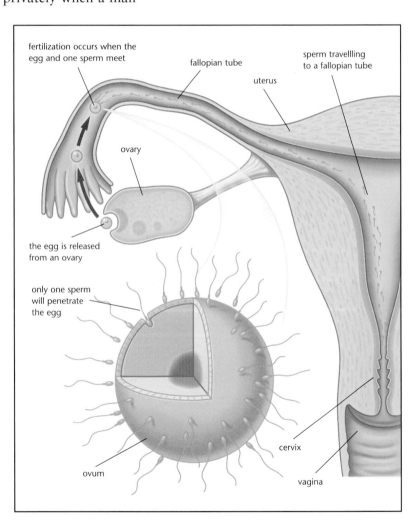

fertilization occurs when the egg and one sperm meet

fallopian tube

sperm travellling to a fallopian tube

uterus

ovary

the egg is released from an ovary

only one sperm will penetrate the egg

cervix

ovum

vagina

How a new life begins. This diagram shows how sperm travel through the cervix and uterus and into a fallopian tube to fertilize an egg.

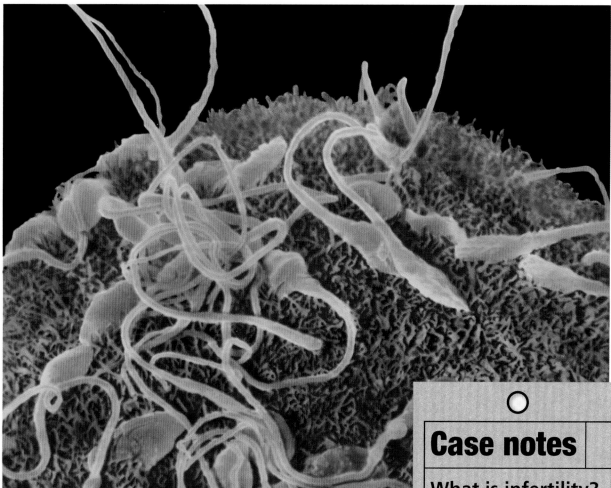

Only one sperm out of the thousands released can join with the egg and start a new life.

Not all the sperm, however, surround the egg. This is because the egg releases a chemical which can attract only about two hundred sperm. Out of these two hundred, only one sperm will join with the egg.

Life is not started every time a man and woman have sexual intercourse. Reproduction only happens if a sperm joins with an egg within twenty-four to thirty-six hours of the egg leaving the ovary for the fallopian tube. Any later than this and the egg is too old. It will simply break down and come out of the woman's body during her period.

Case notes

What is infertility?

Sometimes, despite having sexual intercourse, people cannot reproduce and are described as infertile. The reasons for this can be quite complicated, but usually it is to do with the reproductive organs not working properly. Scientists and doctors have been able to help some couples, who seem infertile, to reproduce. Some people, however, are never able to have their own children and this can be very upsetting for them.

Genes and Chromosomes

Eggs and sperm carry important information and instructions. When the egg and sperm meet at fertilization to form a new life, this information determines how the baby will look, whether it will be a boy or girl and how its body will function.

The information about all these things is contained in tiny packages called genes, and they lie on chromosomes. Chromosomes are coiled strands of a chemical called DNA (deoxyribonucleic acid). Each egg and each sperm have twenty-three chromosomes.

During fertilization, the egg and sperm create one cell containing forty-six chromosomes (twenty-three from each parent) and more than one hundred thousand genes. This cell then multiplies into other cells, each one containing the same forty-six chromosomes and genes.

Genes

Genes decide things like the eye, skin and hair colour of the baby, and how tall he or she will grow. Genes are passed on through families. As well as the genes of its parents, a baby's body will also contain some of the genes of

Each human cell contains forty-six chromosomes, which are made of coiled strands of DNA (deoxyribonucleic acid). Genes lie along the chromosomes.

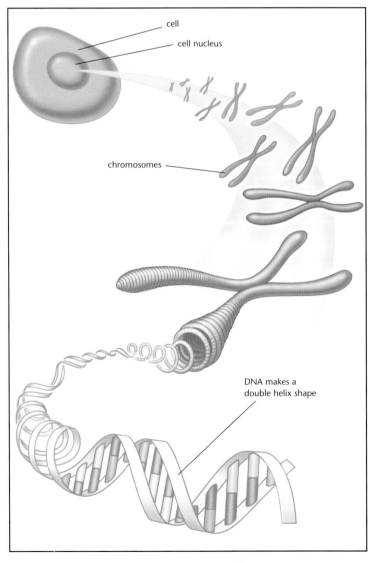

cell

cell nucleus

chromosomes

DNA makes a double helix shape

its grandparents, great-grandparents and even its ancient ancestors. Genes also determine whether a baby will inherit certain diseases. Diseases like cystic fibrosis, muscular dystrophy and haemophilia are passed on through families.

The order in which genes and chromosomes are put together is what makes humans unique – no two humans can have the same DNA. The only exceptions to this rule are identical twins (see panel).

These identical twins were formed when their mother's egg split into two after being fertilized by the father's sperm.

Boy or Girl?

Eggs and sperm contain a sex chromosome that scientists call X or Y. As soon as an egg and sperm join together, the combination of sex chromosomes they produce decides whether the baby will be a boy or a girl. Eggs can only have the X chromosome, but sperm can have either an X or a Y. If a sperm with an X chromosome joins with the egg, then the baby will be a girl. If a sperm with a Y chromosome joins with the egg, then the baby will be a boy.

Case notes

How are twins made?

There are two types of twins – identical and fraternal. Fraternal or non-identical twins form when two eggs leave the ovaries at exactly the same time and are fertilized by two separate sperm. These twins will not look identical and they can be different sexes. Identical twins form if a single egg splits into two after fertilization. These twins will be the same sex, share the same genes, and look the same.

Early Development

After the egg and sperm join, they form one cell. A few hours later this cell splits in half. Then these new cells split in two to create four cells. All the cells keep splitting over and over again until a ball of cells called a blastocyst is produced.

The blastocyst forms more cells as it travels slowly down a fallopian tube towards the uterus. The journey takes about seven days and the blastocyst will be made up of about one hundred cells when it arrives in the uterus. Once there it floats around for about two days until it finds a place in the uterus's soft lining that it can burrow into.

The centre of the blastocyst contains the cells that will eventually grow into the baby. The cells on the outside form a protective layer – a sac of fluid in which the baby will float until it is ready to be born.

Some of the outside cells – those which have joined with the wall of the uterus – also make an organ called the placenta. The placenta provides the baby with all of the food and oxygen it needs while it grows in its mother's uterus. It also provides a way for carbon dioxide and any other waste that the baby produces to leave the mother's

This diagram shows the journey of the fertilized egg to the uterus. As it travels it turns into a ball of cells called a blastocyst.

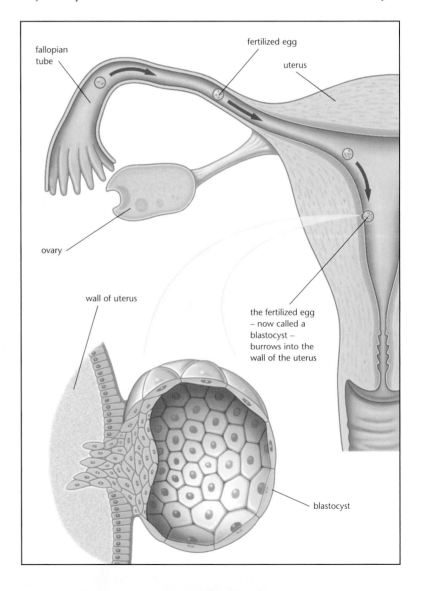

fallopian tube

fertilized egg

uterus

ovary

wall of uterus

the fertilized egg – now called a blastocyst – burrows into the wall of the uterus

blastocyst

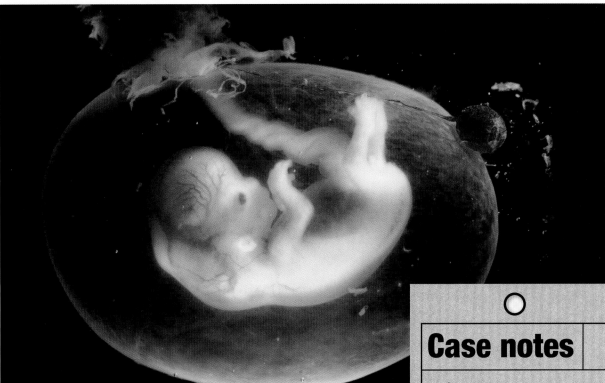

This embryo is seven or eight weeks old. It is just four centimetres long, but its eyes and limbs are already formed.

body through her bloodstream. The baby is connected to the placenta by a cord from its abdomen called the umbilical cord.

For the first eight weeks of its life inside its mother, doctors and scientists usually call the baby an embryo; after eight weeks and until it is born they call it a foetus.

Changes to the Mother

When a woman is first pregnant there are no signs of anything growing inside her at all. Her body is, however, changing. Her periods will have stopped and her breasts may feel uncomfortable as they prepare to produce milk. During early pregnancy many women also start to feel nauseous because of the changes their bodies must make for the baby developing inside. This is called morning sickness, although it can happen at any time of the day.

Case notes

What's a miscarriage?

Miscarriages may happen in the first few months of a pregnancy, usually when the embryo or foetus does not form properly and sadly dies. The uterus then pushes the lining and the embryo or foetus into the vagina and out of the body. For some women this can seem like a very heavy and very painful period. A doctor may decide that a simple operation is needed to clear out the uterus completely. Miscarriages can be very upsetting for everyone involved, but most women who have them go on to have healthy babies.

Weeks Eight to Forty

When the foetus is eight weeks old, it measures around 2.5 centimetres long and weighs just two grams. Its heart and lungs have formed and its arms and legs move about. It is also starting to look a little more like a baby.

At twelve weeks it measures about 7.5 centimetres long and weighs eighteen grams. It has ears and eyelids. At this stage, its head is much bigger than its body. As it grows, the foetus spends its days floating in a fluid-filled sac, called the amniotic sac, in the mother's uterus. Here it is kept at the right temperature and is protected from the outside world.

Taking Care

In these early months of pregnancy, the growing baby can be badly affected by diseases that its mother may catch or by any drugs that she may take. Pregnant women are usually told not to smoke, drink alcohol or take any drugs not recommended by their doctors. They are also often told not to eat certain foods like soft cheeses, shellfish, lightly cooked meat and eggs because these may contain bacteria that can make both the mother and baby ill.

A woman and foetus in the final week of pregnancy.

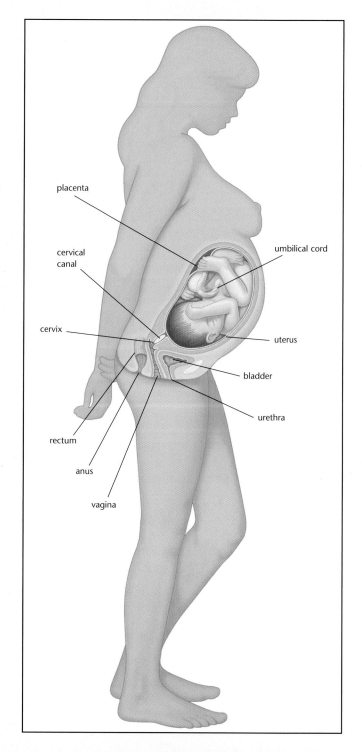

placenta

cervical canal

cervix

rectum

anus

vagina

umbilical cord

uterus

bladder

urethra

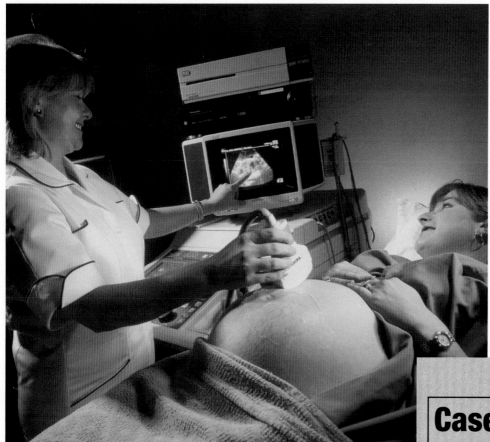

At several stages during their pregnancy, women may have ultrasound scans to check that the baby is growing normally.

The Developing Foetus

Between sixteen and twenty weeks, the baby grows very quickly and its mother's shape changes – she starts to look rounder and pregnant. At about twenty weeks she will probably feel the baby move. At this stage, the baby will be about twenty-five centimetres long. It kicks and somersaults in its amniotic sac and its heartbeat can be heard through a stethoscope. Its sex organs are now also big enough to tell whether it is a boy or a girl.

At forty weeks, most babies are ready to be born and most of them will have turned upside down so that their heads are facing downwards towards the cervix (the opening at the bottom of the uterus). Some babies are born before thirty-seven weeks and are called premature babies. If they are born very early they will need special care at a hospital.

Case notes

What is an ultrasound scan?

Ultrasound scans show doctors how the unborn baby is developing within its mother's uterus. Scans use high-pitched sound waves that bounce off the baby and make a picture. From the picture, doctors can take measurements that show whether the baby is growing normally. Sometimes, if the baby is in the right position, they can even tell if it is a boy or a girl. Ultrasound scans do not harm the mother or the baby.

Giving Birth

Birth starts when hormones in a pregnant woman's blood send a message to the uterus saying it is time for the baby to be born. This message tells the uterus to tighten and squeeze its strong muscles and make a pushing motion called a contraction.

Contractions work together to push the baby out of its mother's body. The time from when the contractions start to when the baby is finally born is called labour. Labour is another name for work.

During labour many women like to have the support of their friends and family.

Hard Work

When labour starts, contractions are weak and spaced far apart. As time goes on they start getting stronger and closer together. It can take just a few hours or several days for a baby to be born. The pains the contractions cause are known as labour pains.

The contractions push the baby's head from the uterus into the cervix. The cervix opens up, getting wider and wider until it eventually lets the baby's head enter the mother's vagina – the birth canal. The vagina then stretches to let the baby out of its mother's body.

During the contractions, a midwife or obstetrician will encourage the mother to push downwards to help the baby out. Sometimes babies need more help leaving their mothers' bodies and have to be pulled out with forceps, which look a little like salad tongs, or a ventouse extractor – a suction cup.

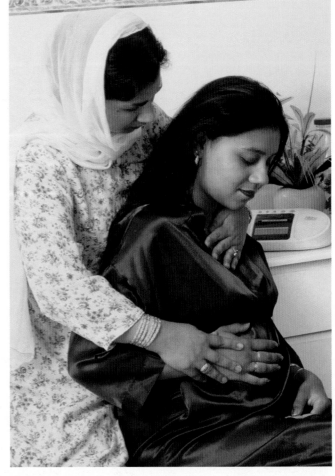

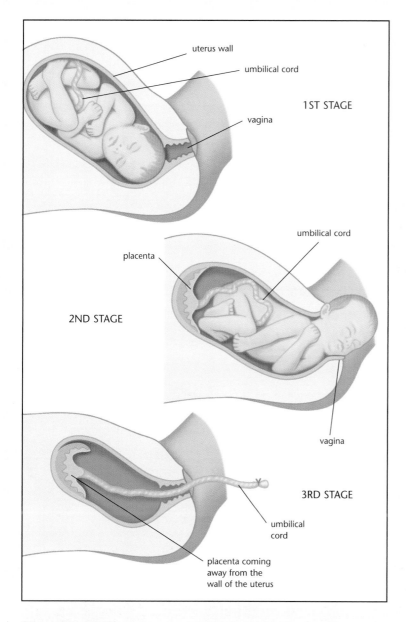

uterus wall

umbilical cord

1ST STAGE

vagina

umbilical cord

placenta

2ND STAGE

vagina

3RD STAGE

umbilical cord

placenta coming away from the wall of the uterus

The three stages of labour.

First Breaths

Once a baby is born, it normally takes its first breath and starts to cry. These cries help to make the baby breathe and take oxygen from the air instead of from the placenta and umbilical cord.

When the baby finally leaves the vagina, the doctor or midwife clamps and cuts the umbilical cord. This separates the baby from the placenta, which at this point is usually still inside the mother's body. Meanwhile the contractions continue until the placenta and the rest of the umbilical cord are pushed out.

Case notes

What is a caesarean?

Sometimes babies are born by caesarean section. This is an operation where the mother is first given an injection to stop her from feeling any pain. The surgeon then makes a side-to-side cut low down on the mother's abdomen into the uterus. The baby and placenta are taken out gently and the cut is stitched or stapled up. Caesareans usually happen if doctors think the mother will have problems giving birth or if they are worried about the health of the baby.

A Baby's First Year

Most newborn babies are about fifty centimetres long and weigh between three and three and a half kilograms.

They can see and hear and will cry when hungry, thirsty or uncomfortable. Babies are also born, like all mammals, with the ability to suckle milk from their mothers. This suckling action is called a reflex – something that is done automatically. If a baby's face is lightly stroked near its mouth it turns its head to one side and opens its mouth. This reflex helps the baby find its mother's breast or a bottle and start feeding.

Breastfeeding is a natural way of feeding babies. Breast milk provides all the nutrients a baby needs to be healthy.

Feeding Time

Newborn babies' digestive systems are not able to deal with solid food, so mothers produce milk in their breasts for the babies to drink. When a newborn baby first sucks at its mother's breast, the hormones in her body tell the breasts to start producing milk. The first liquid produced is called colostrum, which is very thick and full of nutrients. After two or three days of sucking, breast milk then appears. This milk contains all the nutrients a baby needs to be healthy. It also contains the mother's immunities – protection from disease – and can stop the baby getting ill.

Not all mothers choose to breastfeed their babies. Companies make and sell baby formula milk from cows' milk, which can be fed to babies from a bottle. After six months, most babies are slowly introduced to solid food.

This baby is six months old. He can only stand with help from his father, but in six more months he will probably be walking on his own.

Growing Babies

Babies that are healthy and well looked after grow and develop skills. At three months old most will hold up their heads and make noises when they are talked to. They also like to grab at things. At six months most babies will be able to sit up with help and turn their heads around. They can pick up toys and like to put things in their mouths.

By nine months most babies can crawl. They can also hold a cup or bottle; some may even stand while holding on to something. At twelve months lots of babies start to walk and say a few words.

Case notes

How do babies learn to talk?

No one is really sure why or how a baby learns to talk. Some scientists think babies learn by being around other people, listening to them and copying them. Other scientists think that the brain is made so that we talk at some stage automatically. Most toddlers are using simple words when they are between one year and eighteen months of age.

Growing Up

In the first eighteen months of their lives, children experience their first growth spurt, and they grow very quickly. As their growth slows down between eighteen months and five years, they learn more physical skills and become more co-ordinated. From seven onwards, swimming, ball sports, bike riding, dancing and skating all become easier as a child gets more control over its body.

A second growth spurt happens at puberty. Puberty is the time when a child's body starts becoming more like an adult's and when the reproductive organs start growing and getting ready to work.

Puberty

Most girls will start noticing changes in their bodies when they are between eleven and thirteen years old. However, some may notice their bodies changing when they are as young as nine, and others not until they are fifteen. This is all normal.

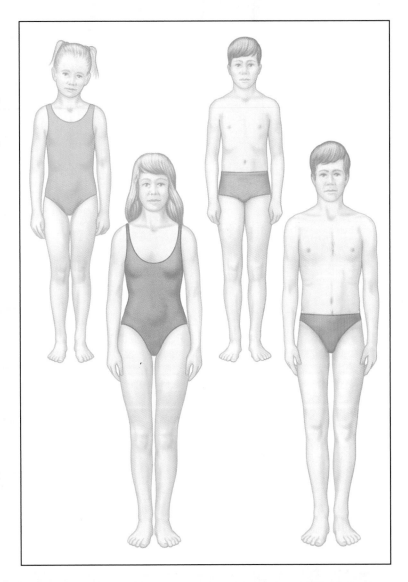

Growing up – before and after puberty.

When a girl reaches puberty, hormones in her blood – oestrogen and progesterone – tell her body to start changing. Her breasts start to grow. She gets a more definite waist and her hips start to look a little wider and more rounded. Pubic hair usually starts to grow in the area between and just above a girl's legs.

Many teenagers get worried about acne appearing on their face, but doctors are often able to help the spots get better.

Case notes

Why do teenagers get acne?

Not all teenagers get acne, but many do. This is usually caused by the extra hormones in their bodies which can cause more oil, called sebum, to get into the pores of the skin and clog them up. This clogging causes bacteria to multiply and this then causes acne. Doctors and dermatologists (doctors who specialize in skin care) can help to make the acne better with special creams and medicines.

Hair grows under her arms as well. Her periods are likely to start around this time, too.

Boys tend to reach puberty a couple of years after girls. Their bodies also change – their muscles get bigger, their voices get deeper and they start to grow hair under their arms and in the pubic area, too. Boys also grow hair on their faces, legs and arms and sometimes on their chests. At this time the male sex hormone – testosterone – is telling the boy's reproductive organs that it is time to produce sperm.

Relationships and Feelings

A human being's world is full of different relationships and feelings. The first relationships babies and children are likely to experience are strong feelings of love from parents, brothers and sisters and other members of the family. They then meet people outside the family. Friends, teachers and doctors are just some of the people that children form relationships with as they grow up.

Relationships that make everyone involved feel trusted, respected and cared for can be described as successful or healthy relationships. A relationship which makes someone feel forced to do something they don't want to do – or that they know is wrong – can be described as unhealthy. Anyone involved in an unhealthy relationship should ask someone they trust for help.

Wanting to be close to another person is a normal and important part of growing up.

Sexual Relationships

Sexual relationships are an important part of being human. Reproduction cannot happen without sexual intercourse taking place and it is natural for people to feel sexually attracted to one another.

It is also normal for these feelings to start at some point during puberty. When the reproductive organs start working, they release hormones into a young person's body that can make them feel attracted to another boy or girl. They may want to hug and kiss them and be as close as possible. These feelings are natural, but they don't mean that someone who has reached puberty is ready for sexual intercourse and a baby.

Sometimes peer pressure from friends and classmates can make young people feel that they should have a sexual relationship before they are ready. Some people may even make up stories about how they have had sex with someone when they haven't, to make themselves seem grown up and experienced.

In a healthy relationship no one should ever feel forced to do something they don't want to.

Case notes

What is a homosexual relationship?

Not all relationships are heterosexual – between a male and a female who are sexually attracted to each other. A homosexual relationship is when two men or two women are sexually attracted to each other. These relationships are sometimes called gay relationships. When two women are sexually attracted to each other this is often described as a lesbian relationship.

Like other successful or healthy relationships, a good sexual relationship is built on trust, respect and care for the other person's feelings. These relationships are built up over time.

Being pressured into having a sexual relationship too early and before both people are ready can result in unhappiness and an unplanned baby.

About Birth Control

Men and women who do not want an unplanned baby can use contraception – also known as birth control.

Condoms

These are a method of birth control that men can use to stop a woman getting pregnant. A condom is a tube of thin rubber, closed at one end. It fits over an erect penis before it goes inside the vagina. Condoms catch sperm when the man ejaculates. Men and women can buy condoms from many different places including pharmacies and supermarkets. They are available free at family planning clinics. There are also condoms for women, which fit inside the vagina. These can be bought from pharmacies too.

Birth Control Pills

These are prescribed by doctors and contain hormones which stop the woman's ovaries releasing eggs. Instead of taking pills, women can be injected with these hormones or have them implanted into their bodies. There are also emergency birth control pills which must usually be taken within seventy-two hours of having sex without using contraception. These are called morning-after pills and can either be prescribed by a doctor, or, in some countries, can be bought from a pharmacy.

Contraceptive pills are a very effective method of birth control, provided they are taken exactly as prescribed.

Doctors are very experienced in giving advice on birth control to young men and women.

Intrauterine Device

An intrauterine device (IUD) is a small, specially designed object a doctor puts into the uterus. IUDs stop sperm and eggs joining together.

Diaphragm

This is a small plastic cap. It fits over the cervix to stop the sperm getting into the uterus. Doctors can make sure that the diaphragm fits over the cervix properly.

Other Methods of Birth Control

The withdrawal method involves the man taking his penis out of the vagina before he ejaculates. This method is not recommended by birth control experts. The man may find it hard to withdraw and some sperm may come out before ejaculation.

The rhythm method of birth control involves not having sex around the days when the egg is ready to be fertilized. This method cannot be guaranteed to prevent pregnancy. The time for fertilization can be hard to predict and sometimes ovaries release more than one egg each month.

Case notes

What is abstinence?

Some couples believe abstinence – not having sexual intercourse – is the best way to avoid an unplanned pregnancy and to show their love for each other. Abstinence means abstaining from or not doing something that a person really wants to do. Many couples who believe in abstinence say that they will not have sexual intercourse until they are married, despite the strong feelings they have for each other.

Sexually Transmitted Infections

Sexual relationships are a normal part of human life, but sometimes they can make people ill. Diseases spread by sexual intercourse or by touching people sexually are called sexually transmitted infections (STIs).

Pubic lice are parasites – tiny six-legged creatures that live in pubic hair. Special creams and lotions prescribed by a doctor will get rid of them. Pubic lice are also called crabs.

Syphilis, gonorrhoea and chlamydia are STIs that are caused by bacteria infecting the sex organs. Both men and women can become very ill from these infections. Infected people can be treated with medicines called antibiotics. Untreated STIs can cause inflammation of the female reproductive organs, which can lead to infertility or an ectopic pregnancy (the development of a fertilized egg outside the uterus, for example in a fallopian tube).

Other STIs are caused by viruses. Herpes is an infectious virus that causes sores on and around the sex organs. There is no cure, but medicines can make the sores go away for a while. Another virus causes genital warts. Although the warts can be treated, they usually grow back again.

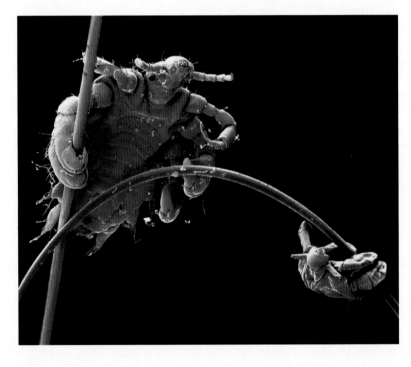

Pubic lice, also known as "crabs", can live in pubic hair and are spread through sexual contact and poor hygiene.

Hepatitis B is a virus that spreads by sexual intercourse, by coming into contact with infected blood, or by being passed from mother to baby during pregnancy. It affects the liver and can make someone who has it very ill. There is no cure for hepatitis B, but there is an effective vaccine (a preparation that can stimulate the body's immune system to fight the disease). Most people who have it get better eventually.

Throughout the world, people are campaigning for and trying to find a cure for HIV/AIDS.

HIV/AIDS

HIV (Human Immunodeficiency Virus) is a very serious STI. There is no cure, although scientists are working very hard to find one. HIV can live in someone's body for years without making them ill, but eventually it turns into AIDS – Acquired Immune Deficiency Syndrome.

Once someone has AIDS they become ill because their body can no longer fight infection and, sadly, they will eventually die.

HIV can live in semen or in fluids from the vagina. It can also be spread by infected blood. HIV cannot be spread by coughing, sneezing, hugging, greeting someone with a kiss or shaking hands.

Case notes

What is safer sex?

Safer sex is also called protected sex. People can protect themselves from STIs by using a condom. Safer sex is also about being honest and respectful in a sexual relationship. People with STIs should always let their sexual partners know and do their best to protect them from disease.

Glossary

AIDS
Short for Acquired Immune Deficiency Syndrome. People eventually get AIDS if they have been infected with HIV – a very serious sexually transmitted disease.

amoebae
Tiny single-celled animals that live in water and soil. Most amoebae can be seen only with a microscope.

bacteria
Single-celled organisms that can cause disease.

blastocyst
A ball of cells which starts forming after a sperm fertilizes an egg.

cervix
The opening at the bottom of the uterus which widens when a baby is ready to be born.

chlamydia
A sexually transmitted infection that is caused by bacteria.

chromosomes
Strands of information contained in the sex cells.

cystic fibrosis
An inherited disease that makes the body create too much mucus.

diaphragm
A method of birth control in which a small plastic cap is fitted over the cervix to prevent sperm reaching and fertilizing an egg.

DNA
Deoxyribonucleic acid is a chemical that makes up the chromosomes and holds genetic information.

embryo
The medical name for a baby during the first eight weeks after fertilization.

fallopian tubes
The tubes that link the ovaries to the uterus, down which the eggs travel to be fertilized.

foetus
The medical name for a baby that has been in the uterus for longer than eight weeks.

genes
Packages of information attached to the chromosomes that decide what characteristics a baby will inherit.

genital warts
A sexually transmitted disease that causes warts to form on the genitals (the external reproductive organs).

gonorrhoea
A sexually transmitted disease caused by bacteria.

haemophilia
An inherited disease that stops blood clotting properly.

hepatitis B
A sexually transmitted virus that affects the liver.

herpes
A sexually transmitted virus that causes sores to form on the genitals.

HIV
Short for Human Immunodeficiency Virus – a very serious sexually transmitted disease for which there is no cure. Eventually it turns into AIDS.

hormones
Chemicals in the body which make things like birth, puberty and menstruation happen.

IUD
Short for intrauterine device – a method of birth control in which a doctor inserts a small device into the uterus. An IUD is designed to prevent a sperm and egg joining together.

muscular dystrophy
A hereditary disease that makes the muscles smaller and unable to work properly.

nutrients
The parts of food, like vitamins and minerals, that are important for growth and development.

oestrogen
A female sex hormone.

parasite	An animal that lives on and feeds off another animal, causing it damage.
placenta	The organ connected to the wall of the uterus during pregnancy that provides the baby with oxygen and nourishment.
progesterone	A female sex hormone.
reflex	An automatic action rather than something that is learned.
sebum	An oil produced by the glands in the skin.
syphilis	A very infectious and dangerous sexually transmitted disease. If left untreated, it can kill the infected person.
testosterone	The male sex hormone, produced by the testes.
umbilical cord	A cord that links the placenta to the baby's abdomen. It carries nourishment and oxygen to the baby.

Further Information

Books

Hair in Funny Places
by Babette Cole (Red Fox, 2001)

Let's Talk About Sex: Growing Up, Changing Bodies, Sex and Sexual Health
by Robie H. Harris (Walker Books, 2004)

The Period Book: Everything You Don't Want to Ask (But Need to Know)
by Karen and Jennifer Gravelle (Piatkus, 1997)

Ready, Set, Grow!
by Linda Davick (New Market, 2003)

Reproduction and Birth
by Angela Royston (Heinemann,1996)

Reproduction and Growing Up
by Steve Parker (Franklin Watts, 1998)

Understanding the Facts of Life
by Susan Meredith and Robyn Gee
(Usborne, 1996)

Websites

www.kidshealth.org/teen/sexual_health/
Contains useful information on all aspects of puberty and sexual health.

www.fpa.org.uk
The Family Planning Association.

www.teenwire.com
The Planned Parenthood League of America.

www.iwannaknow.org
The American Social Health Association.

www.avert.org
An international AIDS charity.

www.bbc.co.uk/relationships/
Contains very good information on STIs and other topics.

www.bbc.co.uk/teens/
Contains advice about sex and relationships.

Index

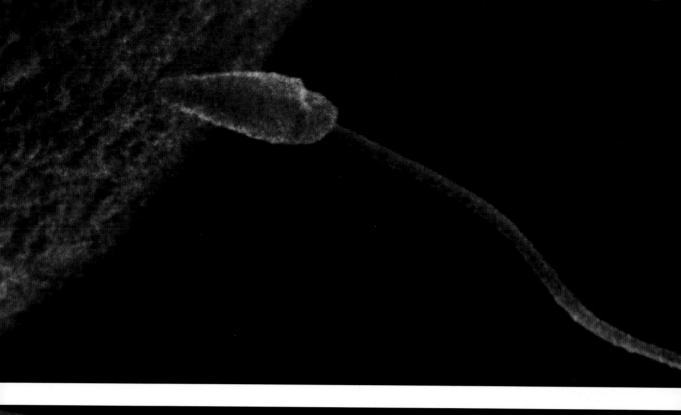

CUTTING EDGE MEDICINE

In Vitro Fertilization

Steve Parker

W
FRANKLIN WATTS
LONDON•SYDNEY

First published in 2007 by
Franklin Watts
338 Euston Road
London NW1 3BH

Franklin Watts Australia
Hachette Children's Books
Level 17/207 Kent St, Sydney, NSW 2000

Produced by Arcturus Publishing Limited
26/27 Bickels Yard, 151–153 Bermondsey Street
London SE1 3HA

Editor: Alex Woolf
Designer: Nick Phipps
Consultant: Dr Eleanor Clarke

Picture credits:
Corbis: 35 (Tomas Van Houtryve), 53 (Shawn Thew/epa).
Getty Images: 16 (Time Life Pictures), 18.
Michael Courtney: 6, 9.
Rex Features: 36 (Action Press), 51 (Mark St George), 59 (Jon Freeman).
Science Photo Library: 5 (Hank Morgan), cover and 11 (D. Phillips), 12 (Steve Allen), 15, 21
(AJ Photo), 23, 25 (SCIMAT), 26 (BSIP), 28 (Pascal Goetgheluck), 31 (Hank Morgan), 33
(Zephyr), 38 (Hank Morgan), 41 (BSIP, Laurent), 43 (John Howard), 45 (Adam Gault), 46
(Andrew Syred), 48 (Mauro Fermariello), 55 (James King-Holmes), 57 (Pascal Goetgheluck).

Every attempt has been made to clear copyright. Should there be any inadvertent omission,
please apply to the publisher for rectification.

A CIP catalogue record for this book is available from the British Library.

Dewey Decimal Classification Number: 618.1' 780599

ISBN: 978 0 7496 6970 6

Printed in China

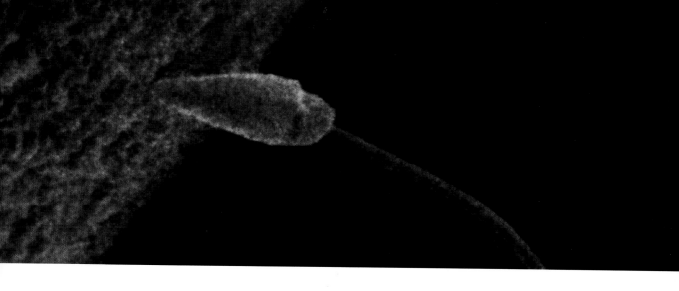

Contents

What is In Vitro Fertilization?

In vitro fertilization, or IVF, is a process in which a woman's egg is joined with a man's sperm outside the body in order to create a baby. *Vitro* is an old word meaning 'glass'. Fertilization is a stage in breeding or reproduction – the process of making babies. IVF, or 'fertilization in glass', refers to medical and laboratory containers like flasks and test tubes. In fact, the container is more likely to be a flat, circular dish called a petri dish, and may well be made out of plastic rather than glass. Even so, the process is still called IVF.

Basics of IVF

IVF is a non-natural way to start, or conceive, a baby. The natural way to start a baby is for a man's sperm to enter a woman's body during sexual intercourse, and for the sperm to then fertilize one of

CUTTING EDGE   MOMENTS

The discovery of human sperm

Until the 17th century, people had no idea that eggs and sperm existed. There were no microscopes to make them visible. Antoni van Leeuwenhoek (1632–1723) was a Dutch textile merchant and amateur scientist. From about 1671 he began to develop magnifying lenses. He drew pictures and wrote descriptions of the tiny lifeforms he discovered in this previously unseen world. In 1677 he described sperm cells from a dog. Later, he observed human sperm: 'A large number of small animalcules, I think it must be more than a thousand, on an area no larger than a grain of sand.' Van Leeuwenhoek's discoveries opened the way to a whole new area of human biology and medicine, including a greater understanding of reproduction.

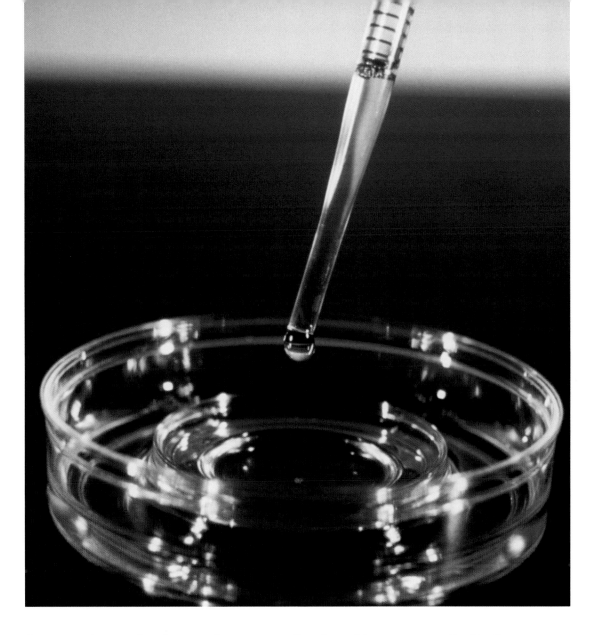

the woman's eggs. In other words, a sperm cell unites with an egg cell to enable the development of a baby. The fertilized egg then develops inside the woman's uterus into a baby, which is born nine months later. For a more detailed description of human reproduction, see pages 6 to 13.

In IVF, eggs are taken from the woman, and sperm is taken from the man. The eggs and sperm are then put together in a container so that fertilization can happen. If an egg is fertilized by the sperm, it is put back into the woman's uterus so that it can grow and develop into a baby. So, with IVF, fertilization happens in artificial surroundings, rather than in a woman's body. For a more detailed description of the process of IVF, see Chapter 3 (pages 20–33).

Droplets of sperm are added to a petri dish containing ripe eggs in order to fertilize them – part of the process of in vitro fertilization.

IVF and ART

IVF is one of several methods known as assisted reproductive technologies, or ARTs. These are scientific methods of helping people to have children. The process of reproduction can be aided or assisted at various stages, depending on the problems of those wanting a baby. In some cases, IVF alone is advised. In other cases, IVF may be combined with other methods (see pages 32–33).

Human reproduction

To understand how IVF works first requires some knowledge of the reproductive process – how humans make babies. This, in turn, cannot be understood without some information about basic human biology.

This diagram shows the organs of the female reproductive system.

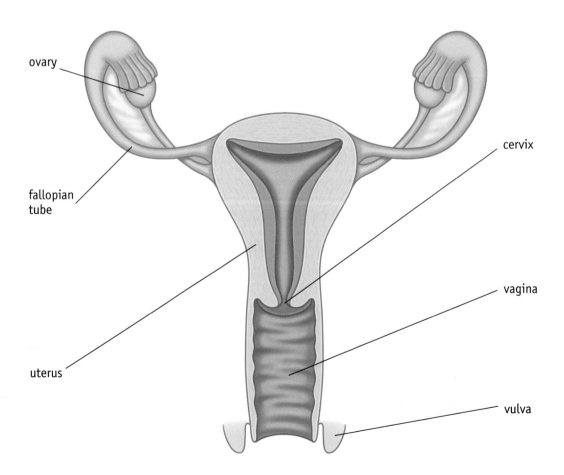

ovary

fallopian tube

uterus

cervix

vagina

vulva

The human body is made of billions of tiny 'building blocks' called cells. There are many different kinds of cell, including nerve cells, blood cells, bone cells and brain cells. Most are so small that 100 would fit on this full stop. Two special types of cell are needed to start a baby. These are an egg cell from a woman and a sperm cell from a man. They are made by the reproductive parts, also called the sexual or genital organs.

Eggs and ovaries

A woman's body contains more than a quarter of a million egg cells. They are located in two organs, called ovaries, in her lower abdomen, one on each side of the uterus. Every month or so – usually every 28 days – one of these egg cells becomes ripe and ready for fertilization. The bodily changes which make the egg cell ripen are called the menstrual, or female, cycle. The changes are controlled by hormones, natural chemical substances that travel around in the blood and affect how its various parts work.

As the follicle containing the egg ripens, the ends of the fallopian tube fold around the ovary to catch the egg. Upon release of the egg, known as ovulation, the female has only about two or three days when her internal conditions are favourable for fertilization. The egg, which is about one tenth of a millimeter in diameter, then begins its journey towards the uterus. Fertilization usually occurs in the fallopian tubes. Whether or not fertilization occurs, the egg continues to move through the fallopian tube towards the uterus.

CUTTING EDGE MOMENTS

Fertility drugs

Fertility means being capable of reproducing. Women take fertility drugs so that their ovaries are more likely to release ripe eggs. The first fertility drug was produced in 1949 at the Istituto Farmacologico Serono (IFS) in Rome, Italy, by Piero Donini. It contained substances called gonadotrophins, produced by a tiny gland under the brain called the pituitary gland. The gonadotrophins travel around the body in the blood and have their effects on the ovaries, encouraging the eggs to ripen. Modern laboratory-made versions of these drugs are now common in all kinds of IVF and fertility work.

Each ripe egg is released from a small fluid-filled container in the ovary, called a follicle. Before the egg is released, the follicle produces the female hormones oestrogen and progesterone. These hormones cause the lining of the uterus, known as the endometrium, to become soft, thickened and rich in blood. This makes it ready to nourish the new baby that will develop from the fertilized egg.

After the egg leaves the follicle, the empty follicle changes into a small yellowish lump, the corpus luteum. This continues to produce oestrogen and progesterone, causing the endometrium to become still thicker, as the egg drifts along the fallopian tube.

If the egg is not fertilized, the corpus luteum gradually breaks down. Without the corpus luteum's hormones, the blood-rich uterus lining breaks down too. This happens around 12 to 14 days after the egg was released. The pieces of uterus lining pass through the opening or neck of the uterus, called the cervix. They then leave the body through a tube called the vagina, or birth canal. This loss of blood-rich uterus lining from the vagina is known as menstruation, or having a period.

A few days later, still under the control of the female hormones, a new egg starts to ripen. Then the whole series of changes that make up the menstrual cycle begins again.

CUTTING EDGE   SCIENTISTS

Gabriele Fallopius

Gabriele Fallopius (Gabriello Falloppio, 1523–1562) was an early scientific anatomist – an expert in the body's structure. By careful dissection (cutting open) of dead bodies, Fallopius discovered detailed structures in the skull, ear and in the female reproductive organs. In 1561 he described the tubes from the ovaries to the uterus, now called the fallopian tubes.

Sperm and testicles

The male reproductive organs are in the lower abdomen and below the abdomen. Two of these organs, the testicles (or testes), produce sperm cells. The testicles hang outside a man's body, below the abdomen, in a skin bag called the scrotum. Sperm cells are tadpole-shaped, with a rounded head and a long, whippy tail. Each day, tens of millions of new sperm cells are produced. They are stored in the epididymis, a six-metre-long, tightly coiled tube next to each testicle.

Sperm leave the man's body by a process called ejaculation. During ejaculation, the muscles tighten in the area of the sexual organs. This pushes the sperm from each testicle and epididymis into a tube, the vas deferens, or sperm duct. In the man's lower abdomen, the two sperm ducts join another tube, the urethra, which runs through the penis. The sperm travel through the urethra (inside the penis) and out of the end of the penis.

This diagram shows the organs of the male reproductive system.

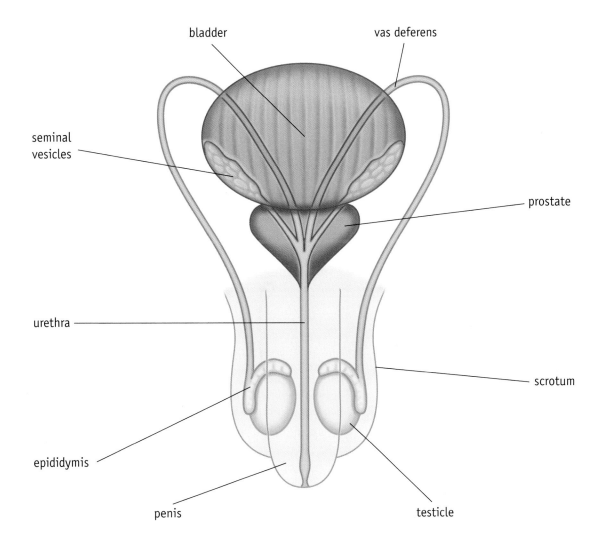

As sperm are ejaculated, a milky liquid called seminal fluid is added to them from glands known as the prostate and seminal vesicles. The sperm in their seminal fluid are known as semen. If sperm are not ejaculated, they die and break apart harmlessly in the testicles and epididymes, and the body reabsorbs them.

CUTTING EDGE   FACTS

Egg and sperm

Sperm cells are much tinier than egg cells, each being about 1/20th of a millimetre long and also very thin. The rounded egg cell, in contrast, is about 1/10th of a millimetre across. The egg cell is therefore hundreds of times bigger, in terms of volume, than the sperm cell.

More than 200 years ago, people thought that there might be a tiny human body curled up in the head of the sperm. The woman's role was simply to provide a uterus for this body to grow. We now know that both egg and sperm contribute the same amount of genetic material, or DNA, to the new baby.

Sex

During sexual intercourse, ejaculation pushes the semen along the man's urethra, out of the end of the penis, and into the woman's vagina. There are usually 200 million or more sperm in a teaspoonful of fluid. They lash their tails and swim from the vagina through the opening of the uterus – the cervix – into the uterus itself. They swim on, into the two fallopian tubes, left and right.

Fertilization

If a ripe egg is waiting in one of the fallopian tubes, the sperm surround it. The sperm continually bombard the egg until one finally penetrates the egg's membrane, or outer covering. The membrane opens and the substances in the sperm's head pass into the egg cell. These substances include the genetic material, DNA. It carries a set of instructions, genes, for how the egg will grow and develop into a baby, a child and then an adult. The egg also has a set of genetic instructions. These two sets of genes come together, one from the sperm and one from the egg, to form the genes of the new baby. This is fertilization.

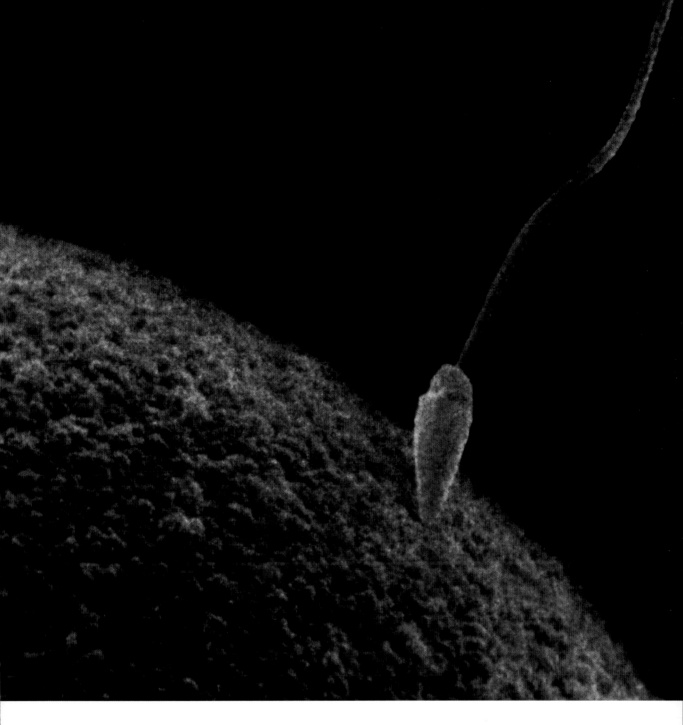

A man can usually release sperm at any time. But a woman only produces a ripe egg once every 28 days or so, and this egg is ready to be fertilized for just two or three days after its release. Also, the sperm live for only two or maybe three days inside the female body. This is why the timing of sex is important for couples who are trying to have a baby. To be successful, they need to get egg and sperm together in the right place at the right time.

A micrograph (a photo taken using a microscope) of a human sperm fertilizing an egg. Of the millions of sperm released by the man, only a few hundred survive the journey to the egg, and of these only one sperm can actually fertilize the egg.

Embryo

Some hours after egg and sperm join, the fertilized egg divides, or splits in half, to make two cells. A few hours later the same thing happens again, forming four cells, then eight cells, 16 and so on. This first stage in development is called the early embryo. It is a tiny cluster of cells that drifts slowly along the fallopian tube to the uterus.

The embryo's cells continue to multiply. A few days after fertilization, there are hundreds of cells. Some of the outer cells begin to make a hormone called hCG, human chorionic

A human embryo at five weeks old. At this stage its eyes and ears have started to form, and the hands and feet have fingers and toes. It is about 10 millimetres in length.

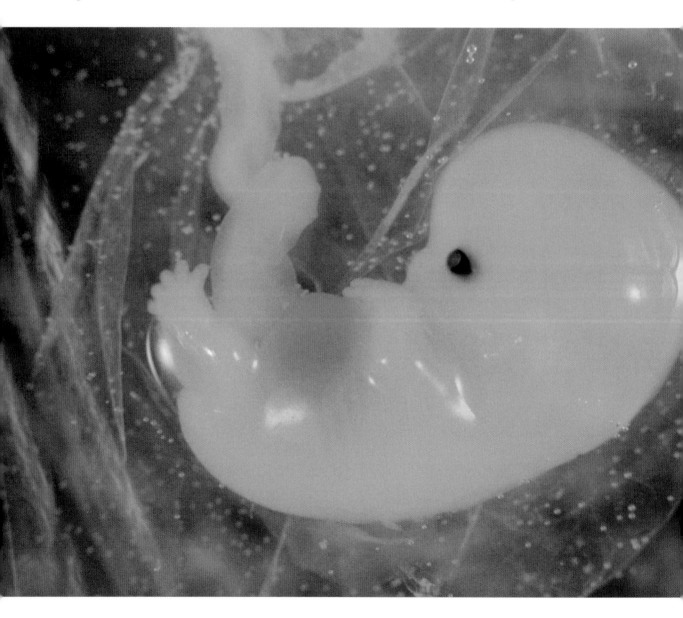

gonadotrophin. Its effect is to make the corpus luteum in the ovary keep producing its hormones, oestrogen and progesterone. This ensures that the uterus lining stays thick and blood-rich.

About a week after fertilization, the early embryo implants (sinks) into the soft lining of the uterus. The lining is rich in blood and nourishment for the embryo's fast-multiplying cells. These cells start to move around, become different, and shape the tiny beginnings of the baby's body, such as the brain, heart and stomach.

About two months after fertilization, the embryo is about the size of a large grape. Yet all its main body parts are formed and its heart is beating.

Fetus

From two months after fertilization until birth, the developing baby is known as a fetus. It grows rapidly in size, is able to move about inside the uterus, and develops the finishing touches to its body, like eyebrows, fingernails and toenails. Finally, nine months after fertilization, the fetus is ready to leave the uterus. It passes through the uterus's neck, or cervix, and along the vagina (birth canal). At last it emerges into the outside world – and a baby is born.

CUTTING EDGE   FACTS

Ultrasound scanners

In the 1950s, it became possible for parents to 'see' their unborn child in the uterus, using the newly developed ultrasound scanner. A probe on this device sends out ultrasound waves (sound waves that are too high-pitched for our ears to hear). When the scanner's probe is applied to a pregnant woman's abdomen, different parts of the fetus's body bounce back or reflect the waves in different ways. The reflections are analysed by computer to form an image of the fetus. Through the 1970s, ultrasound scans gradually became routine during pregnancy. Ultrasound scans also started to be used in all kinds of fertility work. For example, they can be used to check a woman's internal anatomy for abnormalities that might prevent her from conceiving. These might include misshapen fallopian tubes, missing ovaries or abnormal growths. Improvements to ultrasound continue, making it possible to see tiny details of ripe egg follicles and early embryos.

Pioneers of IVF

Medical scientists have understood the process of human reproduction in its entirety for less than 100 years. Yet attempts to help people who could not have children go back way before this time. About 1,800 years ago, in the Middle East, doctors wondered whether a woman could become pregnant if sperm-containing semen was placed in her vagina artificially, rather than by normal sex. Today, this process is known as artificial insemination, or AI.

Gradually, the technique of AI was tried out in animals. About 500 years ago, Arab horse breeders were using AI, and by 300 years ago it was being carried out on reptiles and dogs. AI was commonly used on farm animals throughout the last century. The first human baby born by AI may have been in 1785, but this was an isolated case (see panel).

Increasing knowledge

The early 1900s saw important advances in understanding the female cycle, especially its hormones and how eggs ripened. The details and timing of the cycle were described in 1936 by Carl Hartman of the Carnegie Institute in Baltimore, USA. He showed that for most of the female cycle, a baby could not be conceived. The most fertile time (the time when the woman is most capable of reproducing) occurs just after the ripe egg is released from the ovary.

CUTTING EDGE MOMENTS

The first baby born by AI

The first clear report of assisted reproduction in humans, using AI, occurred in 1785. Scottish surgeon John Hunter examined a male patient whose urethra (the tube through the penis) was misshapen. He suggested to the man that he collect his semen and he and his wife use a syringe to put the semen into her reproductive tract. The couple had a baby later that year. Since at that time people did not know about the female cycle and the importance of timing, the couple were very lucky. Similar attempts at AI followed between the latter 18th and early 20th centuries, but almost all failed.

Lazzaro Spallanzani (1729–1799) was an Italian biologist and pioneer of artificial insemination. He achieved AI in amphibians, insects and dogs.

Hartman's work led to more attempts at human AI, with much greater success. By 1941, more than 10,000 women had conceived by AI. But for some couples who wished to use AI, the man could not produce enough sperm, or enough healthy sperm. This led to the practice of AID, or artificial insemination by donor. In AID, another man, who is not the woman's partner, donates (provides) enough healthy sperm for conception (the fertilization of one of her eggs). The donor may be known to the couple or anonymous (his identity kept secret).

More and more methods

In 1949, Piero Donini discovered fertility drugs, and the first baby conceived with the help of these drugs was born in 1962. Others quickly followed. The popular term 'test-tube babies' was applied to children conceived by this method. Some 25 years later, the same term would be used for IVF babies.

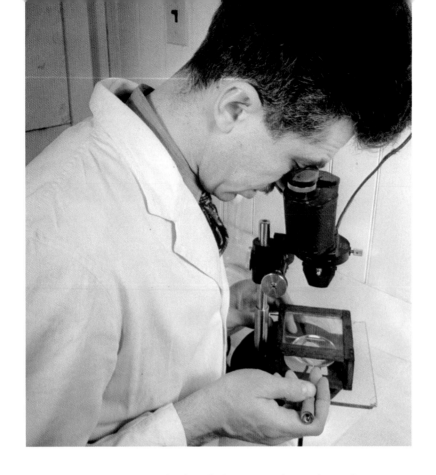

American biologist Dr Gregory Pincus (1903–1967) made headlines in 1934 by achieving IVF in rabbits. The idea of IVF shocked many people at the time, and the controversy threatened Pincus's career.

Meanwhile, in 1954, the first babies were born through AI using frozen sperm. This technique allowed batches of donated sperm to be frozen and then used later, with the identity of the donor kept secret. Gradually, doctors were extending the range of methods to assist reproduction, which now included AI, AID, AID using frozen sperm, and fertility drugs.

First external fertilization

The early methods for assisting reproduction helped large numbers of couples who previously could not conceive. But the methods did not suit many others, who had different fertility problems. For example, women with blocked fallopian tubes could not be helped by AI. So doctors and medical workers continued their research to help these patients.

In 1944, at Harvard University, USA, a doctor and reproductive specialist called John Rock began a new line of research aimed at fertilizing an egg outside the human body – the first attempts at IVF. His experiments failed, but in the 1960s, fertility researchers began to wonder again about Rock's work and the possibility of IVF. In 1969, Robert Edwards, a fertility researcher at Cambridge

University, UK, experimented by placing eggs in a fluid called a culture medium, containing carefully chosen nutrients and chemicals to recreate the conditions in the fallopian tube. Edwards successfully fertilized several eggs. He did not keep the fertilized eggs, however, so there were no pregnancies or babies.

Obtaining eggs

In the late 1960s, at the Royal Oldham Hospital in Lancashire, UK, surgeon Patrick Steptoe was using a device called a laparoscope to harvest, or obtain, eggs from female patients. Steptoe used this procedure to supply eggs to fertility researchers such as Edwards. Steptoe was a gynaecologist – an expert in the female reproductive parts. The laparoscope is a telescope-like device inserted through a small cut in the abdomen, used to view organs such as the stomach and intestines and carry out small operations. Steptoe was a pioneer of this technique of harvesting eggs.

The birth of IVF

During the early 1970s, Steptoe and Edwards began to work together to develop IVF. They did not use fertility drugs on their patients at this time. They monitored the patients very carefully, 24 hours a day, and used the laparoscope to remove the just-released ripe eggs. They also tried to improve the culture media in the dishes so that eggs and sperm felt more 'at home'. This would enable the fertilized eggs to survive for longer, with more chance of becoming early embryos.

CUTTING EDGE   MOMENTS

Landmark experiments with animals

Before trying methods such as AI and IVF on humans, most of these techniques were first researched at length on animals. Many have since become routine methods for breeding farm livestock.

- In 1949, chicken sperm was successfully frozen and thawed.
- In 1951, an embryo was transferred from one cow to another.
- In 1952, the first cow was born through AI using frozen sperm.
- In 1959, the first mammal, a rabbit, was born by IVF.
- In 1972, baby mice were born after being frozen as embryos.

In 1973, an IVF pregnancy began in the United States, but it was stopped very early amid much controversy, leading to a complex legal battle (see page 51). In 1975, an IVF attempt by Edwards and Steptoe ended when the embryo failed to grow.

Success

As news of IVF research leaked out, it sparked a fierce public debate. Many people felt that human reproduction should be left to nature and God's will. Despite the controversy surrounding their work, Edwards and Steptoe carried on. One of their patients was Lesley Brown, who had been trying for a baby with her husband John for nine years, without success. In 1977, one of her ripe eggs

Louise Brown, the world's first test-tube baby, shortly after her birth at Oldham General Hospital, Lancashire, UK.

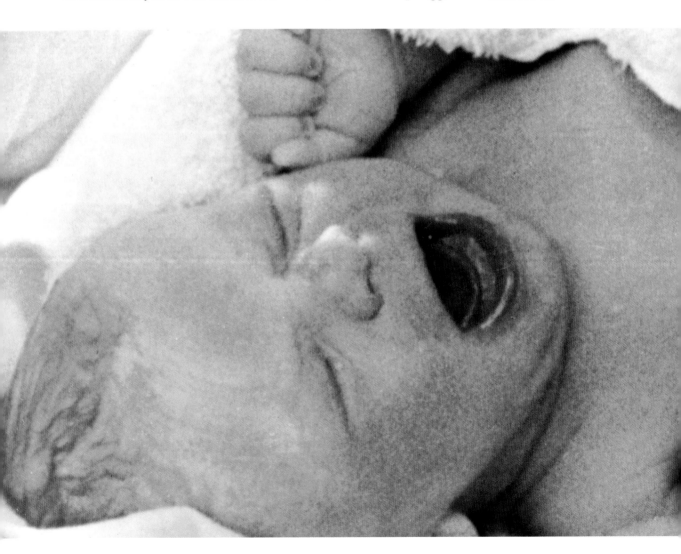

was removed, fertilized with John's sperm, and replaced in her uterus. Nine months later, Lesley gave birth to a healthy little girl, Louise Brown. Louise was the first IVF baby, and Steptoe and Edwards were present at her birth. Four years later, Lesley and John had another daughter, Natalie, also by IVF.

News of the birth of Louise Brown shook the world. As a new type of fertility treatment, it gave hope to millions of couples who wanted children but, until then, could not conceive. However, the event also provoked storms of protest from a variety of people, especially from some religious leaders, who saw infertility (the inability to reproduce) as a condition that God intended for some couples, and viewed IVF as an example of meddling with 'God's will'.

IVF takes off

Soon, other teams attempted IVF, and the number of IVF births accelerated. Twelve of the first 15 IVF babies were the result of IVF carried out at clinics in Melbourne, Australia. This country has been at the cutting edge of IVF research ever since. The first 'test-tube baby' in the USA was Elizabeth Carr, born in Norfolk, Virginia, on 28 December 1981. The Norfolk IVF clinic was the first to be set up in the USA. It was opened in 1980 in the face of great opposition from anti-abortion protestors. (Abortion is the removal of an embryo or fetus from the uterus in order to end a pregnancy.) Over the years, most of the protests died away. Today, IVF is an established medical method, one of a gallery of ARTs – assisted reproductive techniques.

CUTTING EDGE MOMENTS

The first IVF baby

Louise Brown, the first IVF baby, was born on 25 July 1978. Her birth made a huge impact around the world. There was great relief that Louise was healthy and born normally. Today, she lives in Bristol, UK, and works for the postal service. In October 2003, along with many others conceived using IVF, she celebrated her 25th birthday party. In 2004, she married Wesley Mullinder, and Robert Edwards was guest of honour at the wedding. Louise is now pregnant, with an expected delivery date of January 2007.

When and How IVF is Done

IVF is usually recommended as one of several options for couples who are unable to conceive a baby through natural means. Before IVF is offered, however, it must first be established that this is the right treatment for them.

For a couple to be considered for IVF, they must usually have been trying for a baby without success for a lengthy period – generally, at least two years. Their family doctor or general practitioner makes sure that the couple know the basic facts about reproduction. They should be aware of the importance of timing sex around the time of egg release (ovulation), which is indicated by a slight rise in the woman's body temperature. Plotting body temperature on a chart can help to pinpoint this. Kits are also available from the chemist that measure the hormone levels in a urine test and indicate when ovulation occurs.

If after taking the advice of the doctor on the timing of sexual intercourse, pregnancy still does not occur, the doctor will undertake simple investigations to determine whether there is a medical problem with the woman or the man or both. The doctor may carry out physical examinations on the couple to look

CUTTING EDGE   FACTS

Surveys of fertility problems

Recent surveys in countries that carry out IVF regularly show that overall:

- Between 1 in 5 and 1 in 10 couples have problems conceiving a baby. (This is sometimes called infertility, but many of them can be fertile with ARTs.)
- About one-third to two-fifths of these cases involve mainly the man and are known as male factor infertility.
- A similar number involve mainly the woman and are known as female factor infertility.
- In about one-quarter to one-tenth of cases both the woman and man are involved.
- In the remaining cases, usually one-tenth, the exact problem cannot be found. These are known medically as idiopathic cases, but even so, IVF is sometimes successful.

for signs of a medical condition that may have caused one or both to become infertile (unable to reproduce). Problems might include a previous injury or infection of the reproductive parts. In some cases a psychological (mind-related) difficulty – such as depression in a man leading to a lack of sex drive and inability to ejaculate – may be the main stumbling block to conceiving a baby.

Fertility checks

Depending on the results of these early checks and examinations, the couple are usually offered an appointment at a hospital or fertility clinic, perhaps with further tests to try to find the cause of the problem. These include checks on hormone levels – if these are too low in a woman, ripe eggs are not released; if they are too low in a man, ripe sperm do not form.

A couple consult with a fertility specialist. It is important to try to establish the cause of infertility before deciding whether to go ahead with IVF or some other form of assisted reproduction.

Medical staff also check for evidence of infections or abnormalities, which may have caused swelling or scar tissue in the reproductive parts, blocking the tubes that carry eggs or sperm.

The man's semen is observed under a microscope to check the number of sperm in a certain volume of seminal fluid. If there are fewer than a certain number, this is called having a low sperm count (see pages 24–25), and it makes conception by the natural method very unlikely.

CUTTING EDGE FACTS

Allergy to sperm

In some cases, the problem may not be a lack of fertility. The woman may develop a problem similar to an allergy, in which her body reacts against her partner's sperm. Doctors can identify this allergy by finding substances called sperm antibodies in her blood (antibodies are substances produced by the body to help protect it from disease). In such cases, the best solution might be to use donated sperm from another man.

Female infertility

There can be many reasons for infertility in women. These reasons are collectively known as female factor infertility. Some women may be infertile because they have a condition that affects their fallopian tubes (oviducts), preventing eggs and sperm from passing through them or surviving within them. Such tubal problems may result from abnormal development when the woman was young, causing the tubes to be absent or malformed. The tubes may be scarred, twisted or blocked due to infection, injury, a previous operation or an ectopic pregnancy. In an ectopic pregnancy, an early embryo develops in the fallopian tube rather than in the uterus. This damages the tube and causes a serious problem that usually requires surgery.

Infection of the fallopian tubes, sometimes given the general name of pelvic inflammatory disease (PID), is the commonest cause of tubal obstruction. In certain cases an operation can open up the tube so that eggs can pass along it, but IVF is another option. Tubal problems affect about one-third of women who cannot conceive in the usual way.

Endometriosis is a disease of the female reproductive system in which patches or lumps resembling the endometrium (the lining of the uterus) are found in other parts of the abdominal area. The patches thicken and bleed with the menstrual cycle, just like the uterus lining. About a third of women suffering from endometriosis have difficulty in conceiving. The disease also increases the risk of an ectopic pregnancy.

Women may also suffer from other conditions that can cause infertility. These include uterine fibroids, which are lumps or growths in the uterus, either on the outside or inside of its muscular wall, or within the wall's thickness. They may also have polyps – small growths the size and shape of grapes, usually on the lining of the uterus's neck, the cervix.

This colour X-ray of a patient's fallopian tubes shows the left tube (on the right in the photo) to be blocked near the uterus (the central triangular object), causing a swelling in the tube.

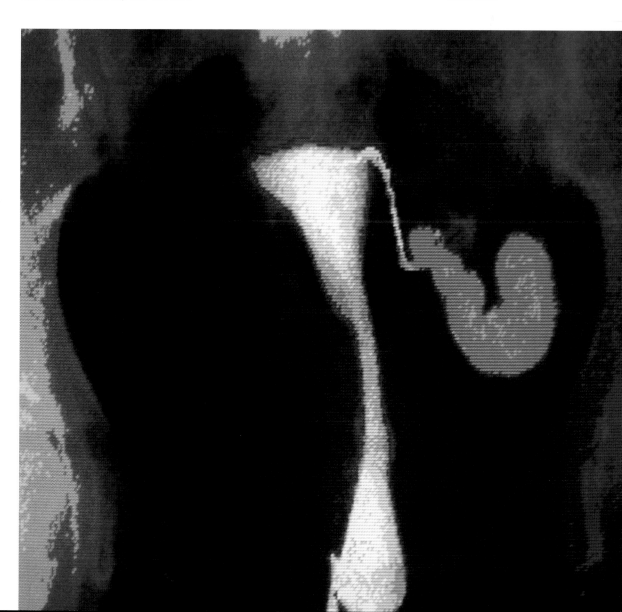

Uterine fibroids and polyps affect the conditions and balance of natural chemicals within the uterus, making it difficult for sperm to pass through or for the early embryo to implant there. Women may have an ovarian cyst – a fluid-filled bag or sac that grows within the ovary and can disrupt the ovary's production of female hormones.

In rare cases, a woman may have no ovaries, or the ovaries lack eggs. In these cases, IVF may still be possible using donated eggs. IVF has also helped post-menopausal women (women who have reached the age when they have stopped menstruating) to become mothers (see page 36–37).

Male infertility

As with women, there is a range of reasons for infertility in men. These reasons are collectively known as male factor infertility. In some men, the testicles produce no sperm, even though the rest of the reproductive organs work well, look normal and make seminal fluid. Another possibility is that a large proportion of the sperm may be malformed: they might lack tails, have two heads or a 'kinked neck'. They may swim around in circles rather than in a straight line.

Some men do not produce enough sperm. This is known as having a low sperm count, and the condition is called oligospermia. A low sperm count is usually measured as being less than 20 million sperm per millilitre of semen. Sperm production can be affected by several factors. Smoking, drinking alcohol, taking drugs, catching an infection such as mumps, and high levels of stress and anxiety can all cause a lowering of the sperm count. Even wearing underwear that is too tight can cause this condition. The testicles

CUTTING EDGE   SCIENCE

Sperm production and obesity

A medical study in 2005 showed clearly for the first time that sperm production is affected by obesity. The more obese a man is, the more likely his sperm will have 'fragmented DNA'. This means that the genetic material (called DNA) inside the sperm is broken or in pieces. Sperm with fragmented DNA are less likely to fertilize an egg, and if they do, there is a higher chance of the embryo being malformed.

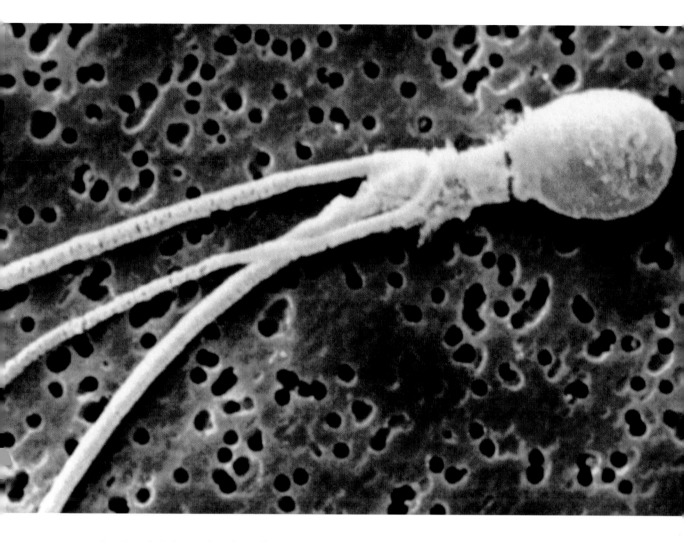

need to be slightly cooler than the main body temperature to work effectively, and tight undergarments hold them close to the lower abdomen and can cause them to become too warm.

A lack or imbalance of male hormones, exposure to some kinds of radiation or toxic substances such as lead or mercury, and certain medications, such as drugs used against the disease cancer, can also cause a reduction in sperm production.

Sometimes the problem may not lie with the sperm themselves. The tubes that the sperm pass along may be absent or malformed. They might be scarred or blocked by an injury, a previous operation, an infection such as cystitis or a sexually transmitted disease (a disease, such as gonorrhoea, that is passed from one person to another through sexual intercourse).

This sperm has three tails instead of the usual one. Deformed sperm can lead to male infertility. In this case, the sperm's mobility may be hindered by having several tails. There are many possible causes of deformed sperm, including blockages in the sperm tubes or sexually transmitted diseases.

25

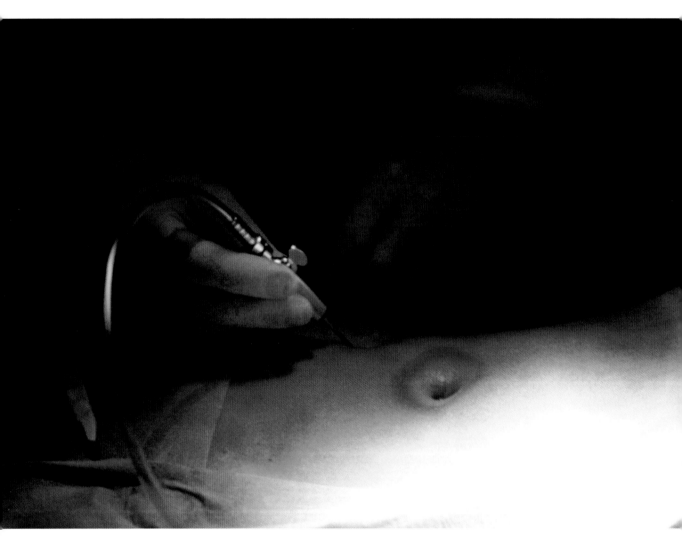

Is IVF the right solution?

When the problem has been diagnosed (identified), the couple and their doctor can discuss suitable treatment. This may be fertility drugs, AI (artificial insemination), IVF or perhaps a different solution such as adoption.

Once the couple and their doctor have agreed that IVF is the best solution, the doctor explains the process to them in detail. The procedures, risks and chances of success are made clear (see Chapter 5 for more information about the risks and chances of success). The couple must sign permission documents and consent forms. Their doctor may recommend interviews with counsellors and psychologists. These experts can assess how the couple will be

A surgeon inserts an instrument called a laparoscope into a woman's abdomen to obtain her eggs. The laparoscope is linked to a video camera so the surgeon can see the ovaries.

able to cope with the stress and worry involved in IVF, especially the disappointment of failure.

The stages of IVF

Standard IVF treatment has four main stages. These are:

- Obtaining the eggs.
- Obtaining the sperm.
- Bringing the two together so fertilization and early embryo development take place.
- Placing the early embryo in the woman's uterus.

Obtaining the eggs Depending on the woman's condition, she may be producing ripe eggs naturally or not. The ripe follicle (the small fluid-filled container in the ovary that releases the egg) can be seen on a detailed vaginal ultrasound scan, using a probe placed inside the vagina, near the ovaries. The woman's progress through her menstrual cycle can also be followed, using a temperature chart and with blood tests to check hormone levels, so doctors can predict when a ripe egg will be released.

When the egg is ripe and ready for release, the doctor uses a needle to suck up, or aspirate, the egg and its fluid in the follicle, usually through the vagina wall, guided by the ultrasound image. The doctor then checks the fluid using a microscope to make sure an egg is present.

CUTTING EDGE   SCIENCE

Making eggs and sperm from body cells

Since about 1995, researchers have tried to make egg and sperm cells from the types of unspecialized cells known as stem cells (see page 49). Animal experiments show that if certain kinds of stem cells are placed together and 'fed' a particular mix of chemicals, they clump into groups similar to the follicles in the ovary. Gradually one cell grows larger and undergoes the special type of cell division that produces an egg. In 2005, similar experiments used an animal's ordinary body cells rather than stem cells. This work suggests that it may one day be possible to help people who cannot produce eggs or sperm to become parents by producing egg and sperm cells from their own body cells.

A technician uses a pipette and a microscope to prepare a human egg cell for IVF. The outer layer of cells, known as the *corona raiata*, are being removed from the egg to help fertilization.

Each course of IVF treatment is carefully tailored to the individual woman, the timing of her fertility cycle and her particular hormone levels. In general, most women receive a series of artificial hormones and medical drugs designed to produce several ripe eggs in the best condition, at the best time, for the greatest chance of fertlization. Some of the hormones and medical drugs are given by injection, others as a nasal spray or tablets. The number and timing of doses is worked out in discussion with the medical team, usually with doses every day or two.

The treatment aims to make several eggs (up to a dozen) ripen at the same time, which is called super-ovulation. This is because having several eggs to mix with sperm gives more chance of at least one embryo forming after fertilization. Also, the hormonal and drug treatments may have side effects (see page 44). So if several eggs are obtained from one cycle, these can be used for more than one attempt at IVF (should the first one fail), and the woman has to undergo only one session of hormonal and drug treatment.

During this time, the woman's menstrual cycle is monitored by blood tests and body temperature readings. As the expected time of egg release approaches, she may receive a 'trigger' injection. This contains a hormone that triggers or causes release of the eggs at a fairly exact time, usually 36 hours after the injection. Knowing when egg release will take place allows the woman and her medical team to plan for collecting the eggs. This is an improvement on earlier forms of IVF, before the use of trigger injections, when eggs might be released at almost any time, including the middle of the night.

Obtaining the sperm Sperm can be obtained by self-stimulation, or masturbation. This involves rubbing the penis until the semen emerges by ejaculation, as it would during normal sexual intercourse. Sometimes this method is not possible because the vas deferens (sperm tubes) are blocked, for example, by a previous injury or infection. In such cases there are a number of methods, known collectively as surgical sperm collection (SSC).

For example, sperm can be obtained from the epididymis, the coiled tube next to the testicle where the sperm are stored. The doctor makes small cuts in the scrotum and epididymis and the sperm are gently squeezed out or sucked up through a needle.

CUTTING EDGE MOMENTS

IVF firsts
After the birth of Louise Brown, many other IVF firsts followed:
- **1982** The first test-tube twins were born in the UK to parents Jo and Stewart Smith. (The tendency today is to avoid multiple births as they increase the risk of complications – see page 42.)
- **1983** In Australia, the first baby was born after freezing the embryo, then thawing and transferring it to the uterus.
- **1984** A woman in Australia with no ovaries gave birth using IVF, donor eggs and hormone treatment.

Once the sperm are obtained, the IVF team must capacitate them. Capacitation is a process that happens to sperm after they enter the woman's body during sexual intercourse. The front end, or 'cap', of the sperm changes in consistency so it will be ready to join with the egg when it makes contact, and the sperm's outer membrane also alters, becoming more flexible, so the sperm can swim more effectively. Capacitation makes fertilization of the egg much more likely. The IVF team mimic the conditions experienced by the sperm during sexual intercourse by adding various chemicals to the culture fluid and carefully controlling the temperature, so that the sperm become capacitated.

Mixing eggs and sperm The eggs and sperm are examined under a microscope and the healthiest ones are selected. Then the eggs and sperm are placed in a culture medium in a dish in a carefully controlled environment designed to mimic the natural conditions in the female reproductive tract. The following day the mixture is checked under a microscope to see if any eggs have been fertilized. If so, the embryo or embryos can be placed in the woman's uterus.

CUTTING EDGE — FACTS

IVF statistics

- Between 1978, when IVF was first successful, and 2005, almost two million babies around the world have been born using IVF and similar ARTs (assisted reproductive technologies).
- In the UK and USA, about one baby in 100 born is conceived using IVF.
- In Australia, the proportion of all births using ARTs is one baby in 50.
- In Iceland, the number is about one in 25 babies.

Before the embryos are placed in the woman's uterus, one or two cells from each embryo may be removed and tested. The aim is to detect and discard cells containing faulty genes that may cause genetic (inherited) diseases such as cystic fibrosis. This testing process is called pre-implantation genetic diagnosis (PGD). For more details about PGD, see pages 56 to 57.

In many cases, unused embryos are frozen, in case the first attempt to transfer the embryo into the mother's uterus does not work. Sometimes, spare embryos are used for research such as work on stem cells (see page 49), although this practice is controversial and is illegal in many countries, including the USA. Frozen embryos may even be stored long term for unknown use in the distant future.

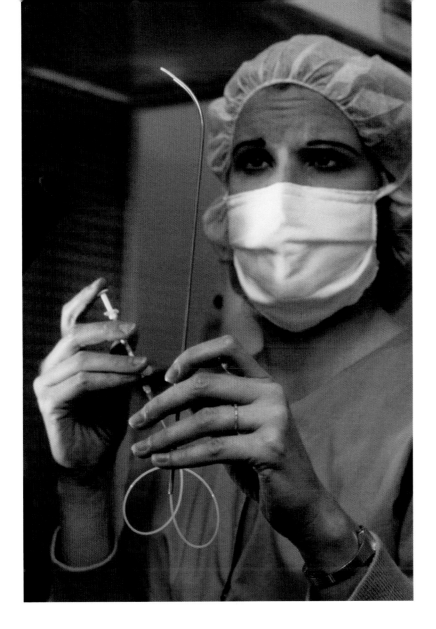

A technician holds a catheter containing several embryos, ready to transfer them into the mother's uterus.

Into the uterus The fourth and final stage of IVF is embryo transfer – the placing of the embryo in the mother's uterus. This is done through a very fine tube called a catheter, which is passed through the vagina and cervix into the uterus.

After the embryo has been transferred, the woman may be given further hormone injections and perhaps pessaries (tablets containing hormones placed in the vagina) to help the embryo implant itself in the lining of the uterus. Blood tests may be used to check that the embryo is implanted and the pregnancy is established. Another ultrasound scan is usually taken to check progress. At this stage, with the woman successfully pregnant, IVF is complete.

Variations on IVF

There are many variations on the standard pattern of IVF, with each couple receiving treatment tailored to their particular requirements.

ICSI An increasingly common variation of IVF is intra-cytoplasmic sperm injection, or ICSI. In this technique, instead of allowing sperm and eggs to mingle freely, a single sperm is injected directly into an egg, using a micro-needle (a very tiny hollow needle attached to a syringe). This can be a useful method if the man's sperm count is low, and especially if there are many abnormal sperm. A normal, healthy-looking individual sperm is selected and taken into a micro-needle. The needle's tip is pushed through the outer wall of the egg and the sperm is injected into the egg's interior.

CUTTING EDGE   SCIENCE

ICSI breakthrough?

Researchers are continually trying to improve methods such as ICSI. In 2005, researchers working on mouse sperm at the University of Hawaii School of Medicine showed that breaking the sperm's 'cap' at the front end of the sperm (the acrosome) may increase the chances of successful fertilization when using ICSI. The acrosome usually pushes against the egg and forms an opening so that the sperm's DNA can pass into the egg. Further tests may show whether this also happens in humans.

Assisted hatching Another variation on IVF is called assisted hatching, or laser hatching. This technique is usually carried out in cases where, for various reasons (which are sometimes never discovered), previous attempts at IVF have failed at the implantation stage. A laser beam or chemical makes a small hole in the outer shell of the early embryo before it is put back into the uterus. This gives the embryo a higher chance of implanting into the uterus lining.

GIFT, ZIFT and TET In some cases, inserting the embryo into the uterus through the cervix is difficult because of, for instance, a very narrow or abnormally shaped cervix, making standard IVF problematic. In these cases, doctors may use one of the following techniques.

GIFT stands for gamete intra-fallopian tube transfer. In this technique, eggs and sperm (which are known as gametes) are collected and checked as in standard IVF procedure. But instead of placing the eggs and sperm into a culture medium, they are put back into the woman's fallopian tube using a laparoscope. Fertilization then takes place in the fallopian tube, as happens in natural conceptions.

ZIFT stands for zygote intra-fallopian transfer. The procedure resembles the standard pattern of IVF, with eggs fertilized in a culture medium. However, with ZIFT, the fertilized egg (which is technically called a zygote) is put into the woman's fallopian tube rather than into her uterus.

TET, which stands for tubal embryo transfer, is similar to ZIFT but more delayed. The fertilized egg is allowed to develop into an early embryo before being put in the fallopian tube.

Some fertility centres and clinics use these variations on IVF when appropriate. However, standard IVF and IVF using ICSI are generally the most common and effective techniques.

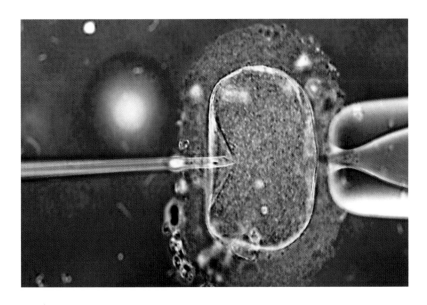

This micrograph shows the IVF technique known as ICSI: a human egg is about to be pierced by a micro-needle containing a single sperm.

Family Matters

In the early days of IVF, couples were interviewed to make sure they were in a stable, long-term relationship, and preferably married. Over the years, social attitudes have become more relaxed in many countries. At the same time, advances in IVF have expanded the range of people who can bear children. Today, many people for whom childbearing may previously have been impossible, are making use of IVF to have children. These include older women, same-sex couples, and even women who wish to have a child using their dead husband's sperm.

CUTTING EDGE — DEBATES

Who should receive IVF?

The overriding aim of the medical teams responsible for carrying out IVF is that the process is successful and that the baby is born healthy. But should they concern themselves with the well-being of those they help to bring into the world beyond these immediate aims? For example, should IVF be offered to a couple with a high risk of inherited disease (one that runs in the family), or to a couple who smoke heavily, drink to excess and abuse drugs? None of these people, if naturally fertile, would be prevented by law from having a baby in the usual way. Should they be barred from having one by IVF if they have the money to pay for the treatment?

Children for same-sex couples

Advances in IVF are creating more options and new situations. It is now possible for a same-sex female couple to use the eggs from one of the women, and donated sperm, to have a baby. A same-sex

male couple can use the sperm from one of the men, a donated egg and another woman, known as a surrogate mother, to have a baby (see page 37). By making such situations possible, IVF has helped to challenge traditional views about what constitutes a family.

A same-sex male couple hold their two-month-old adopted daughter. Today, IVF offers couples like this the chance to have their own children, biologically related to one of them.

Saviour siblings

A child with a serious disease might be helped by a transplant of, for example, bone marrow. The problem with all transplants, however, is rejection. The body's immune system may identify the transplant material as 'foreign' and attack it. Rejection is much less likely, though, if the transplant material is of the same blood and tissue type as that of the recipient. The parents of children with serious diseases, who might be helped by a transplant, are therefore often tempted to have another child who could provide transplant material for the first one. The transplant material would be a very close match, and so less likely to be rejected, due to the close genetic relationship between brothers and sisters.

But if the disease is inherited, there is a chance that the younger sibling might inherit it, too. An IVF technique known as pre-implantation genetic diagnosis (PGD) offers a way out of this difficulty (see pages 56–57). With PGD, one or sometimes two cells are taken from an early embryo and tested for their genetic health. Doctors can use PGD to check whether the embryo will grow into a child with the potential for the disease. Using this technique, the couple can be much more certain that their second child will be healthy and also able to help their older, sick child.

Too old to have a baby?

Most women reach the end of their natural fertile life between the ages of about 50 and 55. This time is the menopause, when the

Adriana Iliescu, aged 67, with her one-year-old daughter Eliza Maria. Some are concerned that women who become mothers at such an advanced age will not be able to offer effective parenting when the child reaches adolescence.

CUTTING EDGE   MOMENTS

Oldest IVF mother

In January 2005, Romanian retired professor Adriana Iliescu became the world's oldest mother. At the age of 66, she gave birth to a daughter following IVF. During a previous IVF attempt, Adriana had been pregnant with twins, but one miscarried and the other was stillborn. This case highlights the risks for older mothers. Opponents to IVF for older women point out that when the daughter celebrates her 21st birthday, her mother, if still surviving, would be 87.

regular female cycle becomes erratic and then fades away. Hormone balances change and eggs no longer ripen. After this, it is not possible to have a baby by natural means.

But with IVF and hormone treatments, it has now become possible for many women over 50, and some older than 60, to give birth using donated eggs. A recent survey showed that post-menopausal women may experience more complications in pregnancy, such as high blood pressure. But apart from that, the chances of having a healthy baby, or of suffering a miscarriage, are not greatly different from those of younger women.

So it is now medically possible for older women to have babies, but what about the family and social implications? When the baby becomes a teenager, the mother may be in her 70s and may struggle to offer the necessary care and support. Similar arguments apply for a much older father.

Who are the parents?

IVF offers people a number of choices about how they conceive and bear children. This can sometimes cause confusion and occasionally legal disputes about who the child's real parents are. For example, IVF allows various alternatives to a woman using her own eggs. These include eggs donated by a relative or friend, or eggs obtained from an 'egg bank'.

Similarly, a woman does not have to use her own uterus. In the course of IVF, the early embryo can be put into the uterus of another woman, known as a surrogate mother. The surrogate carries the baby until birth and then hands it over.

As with eggs, sperm can come from either the partner, or a donor who may be a friend or anonymous. The sperm may be frozen and, like eggs, can be obtained from a local sperm bank, an agency or bought privately over the internet. Since sperm cells can be frozen and then thawed again for use, they can be kept for many years.

These choices make it possible for a child born through IVF to have several 'mothers' and 'fathers'. A baby may be conceived using eggs from one woman, the egg donor, who is the biological,

An IVF technician freezes samples of sperm and eggs in order to store them. Eggs and sperm can be kept at around -180 degrees Centigrade for long periods, and then returned to normal temperature, without causing them any damage.

or natural, mother; it may develop in the uterus of another woman, the surrogate mother; then be cared for and brought up by a third woman, who it knows as its 'real' mother.

Similarly, there can be a both a biological father (known or unknown, depending on where the sperm came from) and a father who raises the child, who it regards as its 'real' father. Or there may only be a biological father, for example in the case of families with a single mother.

Frozen eggs and sperm

It is routine in many IVF centres to save eggs, sperm and embryos for possible later use by freezing them. For example, a woman may learn she has a disease that will affect her abilities to reproduce. She might therefore decide to have her eggs or ovary tissue removed and frozen, so that she can try to conceive later through IVF. Alternatively, she could donate or sell them. For similar reasons, a man can have some of his sperm frozen.

It may happen that if someone dies, his or her partner can use the dead partner's frozen eggs or sperm to conceive a baby by IVF. But legal questions can arise from this. Who 'owns' these frozen eggs or sperm if there is no legal agreement signed by both partners? And if two partners have eggs and sperm frozen, but then end their relationship, does the ex-partner still have the right to use the other ex-partner's eggs or sperm? These situations are regularly tested by court cases.

CUTTING EDGE MOMENTS

Diane Blood

Stephen Blood, a British man, caught meningitis in 1995, went into a coma, and then died. While he was in a coma, a sample of his sperm was obtained and frozen. His widow, Diane, wished to use Stephen's sperm to have a child through IVF. At first the UK's Human Fertilization and Embryology Authority (HFEA) refused Diane permission to use the sperm since her husband had never given written permission. Diane went to Belgium, had IVF treatment there and gave birth to a boy in 1998. After that, the Court of Appeal in the UK reversed the HFEA's ruling. Mrs Blood went on to have a second son, also using her dead husband's sperm.

Success, Risk and Failure

For most people, success in IVF means the birth of a baby. By this definition, the success rate of IVF is around 20 to 25 percent worldwide. In other words, only one in four or five attempts at IVF (known as IVF cycles) lead to the birth of a baby. Many women improve their own individual chances of having a baby by having repeated cycles.

It should be noted, however, that the chances of a couple conceiving naturally during each menstrual cycle are also about one in five. Looked at in this way, IVF is roughly as successful as natural attempts at conception. Indeed, the signs are that over the long term, the success rate of IVF is steadily increasing.

Varied success

The success rates of IVF are affected by a number of factors. Older women, for example, are less likely to be successful. Studies in 2004 and 2005 show that the average chances of IVF success for women under the age of 35 years can be higher than 40 per cent, while for those over 40, the success rate may be less than 5 per cent. Success rates are also lower for women who smoke (see panel) or are overweight. A 2005 survey in the Netherlands showed that being overweight reduced the chances of IVF success by as much as one-third.

CUTTING EDGE

FACTS

The effects of smoking

In 2005, a large survey carried out in the Netherlands showed that smoking cigarettes has a 'devastating impact' on a woman's chances of having a baby using IVF. The survey included more than 8,000 women aged 20 to 45 years. On average, smoking more than one cigarette a day for a year reduced the likelihood of having a baby by IVF by between one-quarter and one-third. Scientists believe that the toxic (poisonous) chemicals in tobacco smoke may affect the lining of the uterus or possibly the casing around the ripe egg, known as the zona pellucida.

Other factors affecting IVF success include whether the eggs are the woman's or donated (donated eggs make IVF success less likely on average), whether they are fresh or frozen (frozen eggs reduce the chances of pregnancy, although with improving methods this is likely to change), and the reason behind the fertility problem.

Overweight women who smoke are stastistically far less likely to be able to conceive through IVF.

IVF success can also sometimes depend on where it is carried out. In some IVF centres the success rate is high, perhaps more than 50 per cent. There are usually background reasons for this high proportion. Some centres only accept women for treatment if they are young and otherwise healthy, and the signs are good that IVF will work.

Some centres have a reputation for tackling more difficult cases. There may be fertility problems with both the woman and man, or they might both be aged over 40. In these cases individual success is less common but all the more noteworthy when it occurs.

More than one baby

As part of the IVF procedure, it is common to put two or even three early embryos into the uterus. This is called multiple embryo transfer, or MET. Experts believe MET allows more chance of an embryo implanting and growing. However, MET often results in a multiple pregnancy, when more than one embryo develops, leading to the birth of twins or triplets. Multiple pregnancies have more risks than single pregnancies, whether the babies have been conceived naturally or by IVF. These risks include low birth weight and premature birth. Because of MET, multiple pregnances are more common with IVF than when conceiving naturally. This makes IVF pregnancies more risky than natural pregnancies.

There is a growing recent trend among IVF practitioners towards single embryo transfer, or SET – putting just one IVF early embryo

CUTTING EDGE   DEBATES

SET versus MET

A European report in 2005 compared about 250 babies born through IVF using SET with 250 single-birth babies from similar backgrounds conceived naturally. There were almost no differences in birth weight or the risk of being premature. Another report, dated 2005, compared SET babies with MET babies and showed that MET babies were more likely to have a low birth or be premature. This was the case even when only one baby was born after MET, the other embryo or fetus having died in the uterus – an event known as the 'vanishing twin'. From the mid-2000s, SET was being advised in more and more IVF treatments, rather than MET.

into the uterus. Some countries, including Denmark and Belgium, are considering making SET a legal requirement. Spare embryos from the IVF session are frozen, and if the first IVF cycle is not successful, a second embryo is thawed and tried in a second IVF cycle, and so on. Sometimes the embryos are kept longer, perhaps for another child in the future, or even as part of stem cell research (see page 49).

These non-identical triplets were born through IVF. With MET, several embryos are transferred into the woman's uterus in the hope that at least one implants and develops into a baby. In this case, three of the embryos developed.

Risks to the mother

IVF does pose slightly more risks to women, in terms of illness and problems during pregnancy, compared to those who conceive naturally. Risks include allergic reaction to certain drugs, headaches, mood swings, hot flushes, vaginal dryness, ovarian cysts, ectopic pregnancy and ovarian cancer. However, these risks have been reduced with the latest forms of IVF treatment.

One potential disorder arising from IVF treatment is ovarian hyperstimulation syndrome (OHSS). This can result from the powerful fertility drugs used during the treatment, especially those that make eggs ripen. OHSS affects around one woman in ten undergoing IVF. The main symptoms are feeling full or bloated, nausea and vomiting, diarrhoea, thirst, dry skin and hair, and weight gain. In more serious cases, OHSS can cause shortness of breath, blood clots in the arteries and veins, pains in the chest and lower abdomen, and abnormally enlarged ovaries, which could rupture or twist (a surgical emergency).

Are IVF babies healthy?

There are many ways of measuring whether babies are healthy. Simple tests include birth weight, reflexes and checking for developmental problems such as cleft palate or spina bifida. Follow-up checks include monitoring weight gain and development milestones like smiling, sitting up and crawling.

CUTTING EDGE   SCIENCE

ICSI study

A long-term study of children conceived using the ICSI method of IVF (injecting a sperm into the egg) was published in 2005. Based in Belgium, it compared about 150 eight-year-olds who had been conceived by this method with about 150 children of the same age and of similar background but conceived naturally. There were very few differences in intelligence and motor skills (movement and muscle coordination) between the groups. In fact, the ICSI group scored very slightly higher on intelligence tests. This may be because they received more attention and stimulation from parents who had to try harder to have a baby and so, arguably, appreciated it more.

Doctors can monitor children's health by checking their growth rate. The most recent surveys indicate that there is no difference between the health and development of IVF babies and those conceived through natural means.

In the past, surveys have shown that, overall, babies conceived by IVF have had a slightly higher proportion of these problems – for example, low birth weight. However, this effect is becoming less year by year.

A major worldwide survey in 2004 tracked IVF babies through their childhood years to adulthood. It showed that, on average, they were as healthy and 'normal' as those conceived naturally.

Applications of IVF

The techniques developed for IVF have applications beyond helping people to reproduce. For example, the fertility drug treatments used in IVF can also be used to treat other disorders of the female hormone-producing glands, which have nothing to do with reproduction. The sperm, eggs, early embryos and methods used in IVF are also useful in many different areas of research, as described below.

A highly magnified photo of human X (centre) and Y (lower right) sex chromosomes. The sex chromosomes that are passed on during fertilization determine an embryo's gender.

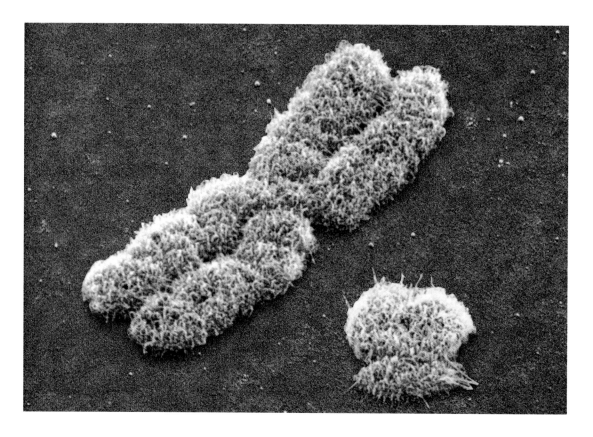

Girl or boy – you choose?

In theory it is possible to choose the sex of an IVF baby. People might wish to do this for many reasons. Some parents may want a balance of boys and girls in the family. In some cultures, parents may prefer to have boys because a girl could prove a financial burden. In traditional societies, women must often provide a dowry (money or property) when they marry, and women have little power to earn their own money or inherit property.

Selecting the baby's sex for cultural reasons or for 'family balancing' is banned in some countries, although sex selection may be allowed for medical reasons – that is, to avoid inherited diseases that only affect one sex (haemophilia, for instance, affects males almost exclusively).

IVF with ICSI makes sex selection possible because it allows doctors to choose the sperm that is injected into the egg. The genetic material in a sperm or egg is contained in 23 'packages' called chromosomes. One of these is called the sex chromosome, and in a sperm it can be either an X or a Y chromosome. If a sperm contains an X chromosome, the baby will be a girl; if it contains a Y chromosome, the baby will be a boy. Injecting an X or Y sperm into the egg will determine the baby's sex. Several ways of separating X and Y sperm are currently being researched (see panel).

An alternative method of sex selection is to allow several eggs to be fertilized as part of the standard IVF procedure, and to test the early embryos for their gender as part of PGD (see pages 56–57). Then only a male or female embryo is put into the uterus, depending on which is desired.

CUTTING EDGE SCIENCE

Sorting X from Y

Researchers have tried various methods of sorting sperm into those containing X chromosomes and those containing Y chromosomes in order to be able to choose the sex of a baby. One recent method is called flow cytometry. A fluorescent dye, which glows under a certain kind of light, is added to a sample of the sperm. It colours or stains their DNA (genetic material). The Y chromosome stains differently to the X one, and an automatic laser-based machine sorts the sperm. This method is improving but it is far from 100 percent accurate.

IVF techniques have been used in the cloning of many animals. Prometea (in the foreground) was the first cloned horse. A skin cell taken from Stella Cometa (background) was fused with an empty egg from another horse. The resulting embryo was then implanted in Stella Cometa's uterus. Prometea was born in May 2003. Stella Cometa was both her surrogate mother and her identical twin.

IVF and genetic engineering

Scientists can use techniques similar to those used in IVF to manipulate the genes of plants and animals in order to make them grow and develop in different ways. This is called genetic engineering. For example, scientists can remove the DNA from the egg of an animal and replace it with DNA from another source. The new DNA might contain an extra gene that will make the animal resistant to a certain disease.

In humans, genetic engineering could one day help to treat fertility problems, or cure genetic diseases. For example, a faulty gene found in an early embryo could be mended or replaced by a normal version of the gene.

IVF and cloning

IVF-type methods can also be used in cloning. A clone is a living thing that is genetically identical to another living thing. Cloning researchers make use of many techniques originally developed for IVF, such as creating conditions that allow early embryos to grow in a container before being put back in the uterus. Many plants and animals have already been cloned.

In humans, cloning combined with stem cell technology (see below) may allow some of a person's cells to be taken and 'grown' into new tissues and organs, as a treatment for that person if she or he becomes ill. At present, the research and practice of human cloning is banned in many countries.

IVF and stem cells

The 'spare' eggs and embryos from IVF are a potential source of stem cells. Stem cells – unlike most cells in the human body, such as muscle cells and blood cells – are non-specialized. Stem cells have the potential to become other types of cell, and may therefore have future medical applications. They could be used to grow tissues such as skin and muscle, and even organs like a liver or heart, from a person's own stem cells. Then, if the person becomes ill, a new tissue or organ could be grown and implanted to treat the illness, with no risk of rejection.

The cells within early embryos, obtained through IVF, are even more useful to researchers than stem cells in adults. This is because most adult stem cells can only develop into a particular type of cell, such as a type of blood cell, whereas embryonic stem cells can develop into any kind of cell.

Rules about using IVF eggs and embryos for this type of work vary from one country to another. Some countries ban their use in any stem cell or cloning research. Others allow the use of embryos up to a certain stage of development, such as four- or eight-cell embryos.

CUTTING EDGE   DEBATES

Embryonic stem cells

The use of embryonic stem cells for medical research has stirred much public debate. Is it right to use an embryo with the potential to develop into a human being as a source of material for stem cell research, even if that research leads to treatments that could improve health and save lives?

Money, Control and the Law

IVF is not just a way of helping people to have babies – it's also big business. The IVF business includes expert doctors, nurses and support staff, fertility centres, hospitals and clinics, as well as all kinds of machinery and equipment. Besides these frontline people and assets, the business is supported by large quantities of promotional material, adverts, brochures, leaflets, training courses, legal advisors, forms and regulations. To pay for all this, IVF treatment costs its recipients thousands of dollars.

In the USA, IVF can cost anything between $3,000 and $20,000 per cycle, depending on a number of factors, including the reputation of the clinic and the 'quality' of the frozen eggs or sperm. ('Quality' is judged on the age and health of the donors.) In Britain, there is far less variation in cost: in 2005, IVF cost a little more than £3,000 ($5,600) per cycle.

Who pays for IVF?

In the great majority of cases, IVF is paid for privately – that is, the people who receive the treatment pay for it themselves. In some countries, such as Australia, people may be able to obtain a gift, loan or grant from a charity or from the government. It may also be possible to take out an insurance policy. If a couple have not had a child after trying for an agreed number of years, the insurance company pays.

In the USA, IVF is paid for privately. Some health insurance plans cover the costs of IVF. Other health insurers have refused to cover the costs of IVF because they do not regard it as a medical treatment, but more of a wish or desire, like cosmetic surgery.

In the UK, most IVF is paid for privately. Only a tiny proportion is paid for by the government-funded National Health Service

CUTTING EDGE · MOMENTS

The first IVF court case

What could have been the first IVF pregnancy, in 1973, instead turned into the first of many IVF court cases. In New York City, USA, Doctors William Sweeney and Landrum Shettles took eggs from patient Doris Del-Zio and sperm from her husband John and mixed them in a test tube. The process was stopped the following day by the doctors' senior boss Raymond Vande Wiele. In 1974 the Del-Zios started a court case against Vande Wiele, claiming $1.5 million. The case was settled four years later when the Del-Zios received $50,000. In 1983 Vande Wiele became a director of New York's first IVF clinic.

IVF has been at the centre of a number of legal disputes. In 2003, two women in the UK, Natallie Evans (right) and Lorraine Hadley (left) went to court to try save frozen embryos, conceived with their former partners, from being destroyed. The former partners had withdrawn consent for the embryos to be used in IVF treatment. The women lost the case.

(NHS). New UK guidelines in 2005 established that couples who met certain conditions should be given three cycles of IVF treatment, paid for by the NHS. Couples must be, for example, childless, under 35 years old, in good general health, and not have a family history of certain illnesses.

Who controls IVF?

Most countries have a government-appointed authority to monitor IVF, establish codes of practice, and ensure that it is being carried out safely and to a high standard. Practitioners of IVF are also bound by national, regional and state laws.

In the UK, the process of monitoring IVF began with the Human Fertility and Embryology Act of 1990. The UK Human Fertility and Embryology Authority (HFEA) was set up in 1991 to oversee IVF and other forms of assisted reproduction, as well as IVF applications such as research into stem cells and cloning.

In the USA, IVF is controlled by the American Society for Reproductive Medicine (ASRM) and the Centers for Disease Control (CDC). In Australia, the National Health and Medical Research Council (NHMRC) oversees IVF.

International organizations include the European Society for Human Reproduction and Embryology (ESHRE) and the International Federation of Fertility Societies (IFFS). Both of these organizations coordinate information from around the world on the latest developments in IVF, and provide summaries to IVF clients and practitioners, as well as to governmental and regional bodies.

Rights and wrongs

IVF remains a controversial technique for many people and has been the subject of fierce disagreement. Anti-IVF campaigners often have moral or religious objections to the practice. Many do not believe that humans have the right to interfere in what is seen as

CUTTING EDGE   FACTS

IVF tourism

The laws on IVF vary hugely from country to country. In some countries in the Middle East it is totally illegal. Other countries, such as Hungary and Slovenia, allow many forms of IVF, and clinics are often unregulated. Most exist somewhere in beween these extremes, permitting IVF, but with strict controls to try make it as safe and effective as possible. Since the mid-1990s, these variations between countries have led to a booming international business in 'IVF tourism'. People seeking IVF treatment often have pre-IVF tests and checks in their own country – if these are not illegal there. They then travel abroad, perhaps even taking the frozen or fresh samples of eggs and sperm with them, to have the IVF treatment. People also decide to travel abroad for IVF for reasons of cost, as prices vary considerably around the globe. In 2005 the cost of an IVF cycle in India could be less than one-fifth of its cost in the USA.

God's will. Some argue that any fertilized egg or early embryo is a human being in the making and has human rights, and they deplore the way IVF teams often simply discard unused embryos.

Others are in favour of IVF and desire even further advances in this field. They focus on the great joy IVF has brought to couples who, without this procedure, would have had no chance of becoming parents. Companies with interests in IVF, such as drug companies and medical equipment manufacturers, also add their voices to the debate. Campaigners and lobbyists on both sides put pressure on legislators and government authorities to change the laws and regulations that govern IVF.

US president George W. Bush at a White House ceremony in July 2006. He was congratulating families who have adopted frozen embryos left over from other couples' attempts to conceive through IVF. Bush is holding Jack Jones, one of these so-called 'snowflake babies'. Many people feel strongly that all embryos have a right to life.

IVF and the Future

IVF is now a well-established medical technique, and, although only about one in four or five IVF cycles are successful, success rates are gradually improving year by year.

The long-term effects of IVF have defied the predictions of its early opponents. The large majority of IVF babies have grown up healthy, and there is no evidence to suggest that IVF has led to a breakdown of family life – although it has given rise to some unusual kinds of family (see Chapter 4).

Current and future trends

IVF is an evolving science. Its techniques are continually being tested and monitored as part of ongoing efforts to improve its safety and success rate. So what is happening in IVF today, and what are the trends for the near future?

Medical advice is certainly turning against multiple embryo transfer, or MET (placing two or three early embryos into the uterus). The current trend in IVF is towards single embryo transfer, or SET, in order to diminish the risks to the mother and to the unborn child.

CUTTING EDGE   SCIENCE

Signalling substance

In 2005, researchers working with mice discovered a 'signalling substance' called lysophosphatidic acid (LPA). This helps the early embryo to sink or implant itself into the lining of the uterus. Medical drugs that mimic or boost the effect of LPA might increase the chances of implanting as part of IVF.

The ICSI form of IVF, in which a sperm is injected directly into the egg, is becoming increasingly popular. In some IVF centres it has overtaken 'traditional' IVF, in which eggs and sperm are mixed in a dish.

Researchers are looking at new ways of making IVF safer and more effective. Methods might in future include pre-treating sperm for use in ICSI to make fertilization more likely – for example, by breaking the sperm's acrosome (see panel on page 32). Researchers are also looking at ways of making the early embryo more likely to implant in the uterus (see panel).

As IVF has become more widespread and established, IVF centres have tried to make the service more convenient and customer friendly. Would-be parents visit what appears more like an office than a medical centre, and can arrange to have their appointments during their lunch break.

Two micro-needles are inserted into a droplet of semen to capture fertile sperm, using a method known as CISS (computer imaging sperm selection). The sperm, viewed through a video microscope, are selected by a computer for their fertility, based on their tail movement – the more vigorously the tail moves, the faster they swim, and the more likely they are to fertilize an egg.

PGD

One of the biggest growth areas in IVF is pre-implantation genetic diagnosis (PGD). With PGD, one or two cells are taken from the early embryos at about the eight-cell stage, three days after fertilization. The cells are put through tests of 'genetic health'. During testing, the embryos are kept in dishes. Following the tests, only one embryo – which has passed the tests and has the most normal, healthy appearance of those available – is put into the uterus.

PGD dates back to the early 1990s, when it was used to detect problems such as Duchenne muscular dystrophy and Down's syndrome. Since then, thanks to the rapid progress in the science of genetics, the number of genetic problems that can be detected by PGD is far greater, and still rising. Almost every month a new gene is added to the list of those that can be checked by PGD. PGD can even detect the sex of the embryo (see pages 46–47).

PGD is used in cases where standard IVF may not be safe or successful. For example, it may be used if there is a history of a genetic disease in the family, or for women who are older, or who have already had several miscarriages (the unintended ending of a pregnancy through the discharge of the fetus from the uterus), or who have not become pregnant after several IVF cycles.

By the end of 2005, over 5,000 IVF babies around the world had been born using PGD. An ongoing survey in Europe monitors about 200 children born after IVF and PGD, who are now in their teens. By the mid-2000s they appeared to be developing in much the same way as other children.

The use of PGD is increasing year by year. A 2005 report suggested that PGD might soon even become a routine method in

CUTTING EDGE   SCIENCE

Predicting problems

PGD may also be used as a predictor of problems with IVF. If all the embryos from one IVF cycle are found to have genetic disorders, this suggests the same could happen for the next IVF attempt. It could indicate that IVF for the woman in question will never be successful. This knowledge, while very disappointing, might save more wasted effort and hope, as well as time and money.

IVF. In standard IVF, early embryos are usually selected for putting into the uterus on the basis of what they look like – how many cells, how intact they appear, and their overall shape. But according to the 2005 report, even normal-looking embryos sometimes have genetic or chromosome defects. And this is the case not only with embryos from the eggs of older women, but with those from younger women, too. In one study of almost 800 early embryos, three-quarters of those that looked normal actually had chromosome disorders.

PGH

In 2006, a team of scientists in the UK announced a new version of PGD known as pre-implantation genetic haplotyping (PGH). Instead of screening cells from an early embryo for just one or two specific genetic defects, PGH looks for particular 'markers' known to occur on chromosomes with faulty genes. It uses MDA (see page 58) to make many copies of the genes fast, for mass testing. The method can identify many more types of genetic problems than PGD in one screening.

An IVF human embryo undergoing PGD. The eight-celled embryo is being held by a pipette (left) so that a smaller pipette (right) can break the embryo membrane in order to remove one of the cells for screening.

Multiple displacement amplification

In 2004 a new process was developed called multiple displacement amplification (MDA). This makes millions of copies of DNA from one cell of an early embryo. MDA, when used alongside PGD, makes it easier to identify faulty genes. In 2005 in Spain, MDA and PGD were used together to screen embryos from the sperm of a man with a genetic disease called Marfan syndrome. Marfan syndrome is a condition that causes curvature of the spine, joint and muscle weakness and other problems.

IVF and 'designer babies'

In a sense, 'designer babies' are already with us. Babies have been born who, as early embryos, have been checked and selected by PGD to ensure they do not have certain genetic diseases. So far, PGD has been used only for medical purposes. But in the future, this technique may also be used for other reasons. The genes of early embryos might be checked for features such as skin colour, hair colour, adult height, even intelligence. In theory, assuming the genes for these characteristics are identified, this is technically possible. However, there may be profound moral and social implications for this kind of selection. The rich, who could afford this kind of treatment, would have genetically advantaged children – healthier and more intelligent than naturally conceived children. In the long term this may lead to a sharply divided, very unequal society.

CUTTING EDGE MOMENTS

The first 'designer baby'

In August 2000 newspaper headlines hailed Adam Nash as the world's first 'designer baby', born using IVF. In fact he had been born using PGD to select one embryo from 15, to ensure he did not have a gene for a rare blood disease called Fanconi's anaemia – and to be a 'saviour sibling'. Adam was born healthy, and stem cells from his umbilical cord were used to treat his sister Molly, who did have the disease.

Personal organ banks

Another possible future development in IVF is the creation of personal organ banks for IVF children. It is possible to split an early

IVF embryo and store some of its cells as stem cells for very long periods by freezing them, while the rest of the embryo develops into a baby. In the future it may be possible to use these embryonic stem cells to grow tissues and organs in the laboratory. Should the person they originally came from require a tissue or organ transplant, the transplant material would be a perfect genetic match.

Molly Nash, who suffers from a rare blood disease, with her saviour sibling, Adam. Stem cells from Adam's umbilical cord were used to boost Molly's immune system, saving her life.

When present is past

Compared to the controversy caused by the birth of Louise Brown in 1978, IVF today causes much less argument. It is relatively safe and becoming more of a routine procedure for couples who cannot conceive in the natural way. Today, the focus for debate in medical ethics has moved onto newer fields such as stem cell research and cloning. Medical science will undoubtedly continue to push back the barriers of what is possible, stirring up new topics for society to argue about. In fifty years, people may well look back at the early history of IVF and wonder what all the fuss was about.

Glossary

abortion The removal of an embryo or fetus from the womb in order to end a pregnancy.

acrosome The front end or 'cap' of a sperm cell, which pushes against and through the outer membrane (layer) of the egg cell during fertilization.

AI (artificial insemination) When sperm cells are put into a woman's body artificially rather than by the usual process of sexual intercourse.

ARTs (assisted reproductive technologies) A range of techniques for helping people to have children when they cannot do so naturally.

biological mother / father The mother who provided the egg for the conception of a child, or the father who provided the sperm.

cervix The narrowed opening or 'neck' of the uterus, which opens into the birth canal (vagina).

chromosomes 'Packages' of DNA (genetic material) inside a living cell, which look like tiny threads under a microscope.

clones An exact genetic copy of another living thing.

corpus luteum A small, yellowish lump that forms from the empty follicle in the ovary after a ripe egg has been released from it and that produces female hormones as part of the menstrual cycle.

DNA (deoxyribonucleic acid) The genetic material, which contains all the information needed to make a living thing.

ectopic pregnancy The development of a fertilized egg outside the uterus, for example in the fallopian tube.

egg A female reproductive cell.

ejaculate Eject semen from the penis.

embryo The early stage of development of an unborn baby, from the time when the fertilized egg has started dividing until eight weeks after fertilization.

endometrium The blood-rich lining of the uterus, which becomes thicker with each menstrual cycle, ready to nourish the early embryo.

fallopian tube The tube that joins a woman's ovary (egg-producing organ) to her uterus, and where an egg is usually fertilized by a sperm during natural conception.

fertile Capable of reproducing.

fertility drug General name for a group of medical drugs taken by a woman so that her ovaries are more likely to produce ripe eggs.

fertilization The joining of sperm cell and egg cell to form a fertilized egg, which then begins to develop into a baby.

fetus An unborn baby after eight weeks of development.

follicle In a woman's ovary, a small bag-like, fluid-filled container that contains the ripening egg cell.

genes A section of DNA that carries the instructions for the way a living thing grows, develops and maintains itself.

GIFT (gamete intra-fallopian tube transfer) A variation on IVF in which eggs and sperm are collected, then put into the woman's fallopian tube in order for fertilization to take place.

hormones A chemical 'messenger' that travels through the blood to affect cells around the body.

ICSI (intra-cytoplasmic sperm injection) A variation on IVF in which a single sperm cell is injected into the interior of an egg cell.

implantation The sinking of the early embryo into the lining of the uterus, to receive nourishment and continue its growth.

inherited disease An illness or health problem that is passed from parents to offspring through the genes.

in vitro A Latin term meaning 'in glass' and which is used generally in medicine to mean something that happens in artificial conditions.

IVF (in vitro fertilization) A process in which eggs and sperm are put together in artificial surroundings so that a sperm can fertilize an egg to start a baby.

laparoscope A telescope-like medical device that is inserted through a small incision (cut) into the abdomen to look at the parts inside and carry out procedures such as collecting ripe eggs.

menopause A time in a woman's life when her menstrual cycle becomes erratic and stops, so that she no longer produces ripe eggs and can no longer have a baby by natural means.

menstrual cycle The series of changes in a woman's body that occur once every 28 days or so, causing an egg to ripen and be released from an ovary, and the lining of the uterus to thicken, all in preparation for conceiving a baby.

MET (multiple embryo transfer) The placing of more than one early embryo (usually two or three) into the uterus as part of IVF.

miscarriage The unintended ending of a pregnancy, when the fetus dies in the uterus and passes out of the birth canal.

nucleus The 'control centre' of a living cell, which contains the DNA.

OHSS (ovarian hyperstimulation syndrome) A group of health problems caused by fertility drugs in some women.

ovaries Two reproductive organs in the lower body of a woman, which contain thousands of egg cells and which produce a ripe egg every 28 days or so as part of the menstrual cycle.

post-menopausal After the time of the menopause, when a woman can no longer have a baby by natural means.

PID (pelvic inflammatory disease) A general name for infections and other problems that cause inflammation of the reproductive and urinary organs in a woman's pelvis (lower abdomen).

saviour sibling A child conceived, usually by IVF, who can provide body parts (such as bone marrow) to treat the illness of a brother or sister.

semen A thick, milky fluid produced by a man's reproductive parts, containing sperm cells, nutrients and other substances.

SET (single embryo transfer) The placing of a single embryo into the uterus as part of IVF.

sperm A male reproductive cell.

stem cells Undifferentiated (non-specialized) cells that have the potential to divide and develop into many different kinds of cell.

surrogate mother A woman who bears a child for a couple, with the intention of handing it over at birth.

testicles Two egg-shaped reproductive organs in a skin bag (scrotum) below the abdomen of a man, which produce millions of sperm cells daily.

TET (tubal embryo transfer) A variation on IVF in which eggs and sperm are put into an artificial container for fertilization to take place, as in standard IVF, and then the fertilized egg is allowed to develop to the early embryo stage before being put into the woman's fallopian tube.

urethra The tube that carries urine (liquid waste) from the bladder out of the body, and, in men, also carries sperm along the penis and out of the body during ejaculation.

vas deferens In men, the tube that carries sperm cells from the testes, where they are made, to another tube, the urethra.

ZIFT (zygote intra-fallopian tube transfer) A variation on IVF in which eggs and sperm are put into an artificial container for fertilization to take place, as in standard IVF, then the fertilized egg (known as a zygote) is put into the woman's fallopian tube.

Further Information

BOOKS

Great Medical Discoveries: Reproductive Technology by Kim K. Zach (Lucent Books, 2004)

In Vitro Fertilization: The A.R.T. Of Making Babies by Geoffrey Sher, Virginia Marriage Davis, Jean Stoess (Facts on File, 2005)

Science at the Edge: Test Tube Babies: In Vitro Fertilization by Ann Fullick (Heinemann, 2003)

Science on the Edge: Test Tube Babies: The Science of In Vitro Fertilization by Tamara Orr (Blackbirch Press, 2003)

WEBSITES

news.bbc.co.uk/1/hi/health/medical_notes/ 308662.stm
This BBC website describes the latest advances in IVF and explains how it is regulated.

kidshealth.org/teen/sexual_health/
This website contains useful information about the male and female reproductive systems.

www.pbs.org/wgbh/nova/baby/18ways.html
This website from PBS looks at the various methods of assisted reproduction and IVF.

Index

Index <small>*(continued)*</small>